LOW-FODMAP
28-DAY
PLAN

LOW-FODMAP
28-DAY PLAN

A Healthy Cookbook with
GUT-FRIENDLY RECIPES for
IBS RELIEF

FALL RIVER PRESS

New York

FALL RIVER PRESS

New York

An Imprint of Sterling Publishing
1166 Avenue of the Americas
New York, NY 10036

FALL RIVER PRESS and the distinctive Fall River Press logo
are registered trademarks of Barnes & Noble, Inc

Cover design by Laura Palese

ISBN 978-1-4351-6146-7

For information about custom editions, special sales, and premium and corporate
purchases, please contact Sterling Special Sales at 800-805-5489 or
specialsales@sterlingpublishing.com.

Manufactured in China

2 4 6 8 10 9 7 5 3 1

www.sterlingpublishing.com

Quick-Start Guide

If you want to begin the Low-FODMAP diet right away, follow these easy steps:

Familiarize

Yourself with the low-FODMAP diet guidelines. See page 6.

Record

Your symptoms using the Symptom Tracker. See page 12.

Stock

Your kitchen and pantry with everything you need. See page 23.

Prepare

Delicious meals using the weekly meal plans and recipes. See pages 36 and 63.

Reintroduce

Specific foods back into your diet one at a time. See page 9.

Customize

The low-FODMAP diet to suit your body's particular needs. See page 13.

Contents

5. Lunch

6. Snacks

10. Desserts

11. Condiments, Sauces, and Dressings

Foreword

Millions of people around the globe suffer from ongoing gastrointestinal (GI) distress, such as gas, bloating, and constipation, or from digestive disorders like irritable bowel syndrome (IBS). If you are among the many who have these unrelenting digestive troubles and food intolerances, then I am glad your hands have landed on this book.

I understand your pain—I've been there myself. After major intestinal surgery, I struggled to identify the dietary culprits triggering my ongoing bloating and GI distress. It wasn't until I learned about the low-FODMAP diet during my research for *The Complete Idiot's Guide to Eating Well with IBS* and *21-Day Tummy* that a lightbulb went off in my head.

For years, individuals with IBS and other functional gastrointestinal disorders have known that something in their diet plays a role in aggravating their persistent digestive distress. But only more recently has the connection between diet and IBS symptoms been clearly identified and researched by the medical community. Doctors were well versed in diagnosing IBS but less adept at fixing the problem, much to the dismay of their patients.

In the early 2000s, researchers at Monash University in Melbourne, Australia, started connecting the symptoms of IBS to the consumption of certain small carbohydrates. Dietitian Sue Shepherd and gastroenterologist Peter Gibson called these carbohydrates FODMAPs. A group of poorly digested sugars and fibers, FODMAPs pull water into the intestine and ferment rapidly in the gut. Through a wide array of research studies, the Monash University scientists discovered that 75 percent of individuals suffering from debilitating IBS symptoms felt better when they minimized FODMAPs in their diet. Now major medical institutions around the globe are studying the role of FODMAPs in intestinal inflammation, incontinence, nonceliac gluten sensitivity, and inflammatory bowel diseases such as Crohn's, ulcerative colitis, and more.

When you think about how FODMAPs affect digestion, the low-FODMAP diet makes a lot of sense. FODMAPs are osmotic, which means they attract a lot of water when they sit in the intestinal tract. When the bacteria, yeast, and other microbes living in our intestines consume FODMAPs rapidly, they create a lot of gas. This combination of excess water and gas can cause your belly to feel like a huge water balloon. For those of you with a quick moving intestine, the excess water can make you rush to the bathroom. Conversely, for those with sluggish intestines, the lack of movement can trap water and gas and make you feel uncomfortably full and bloated. By removing FODMAPs from your diet, you can remove the cause of all that excess water and gas.

There are a few types of FODMAPs, all found in everyday, healthy foods such as apples, pears, onion, garlic, wheat, milk, beans, and more. Many FODMAPs are quite common, and it's not unusual for individuals to consume multiple types of FODMAPs in the same meal. Although these foods are rich in nutrients, they can trigger digestive distress in people who are sensitive to them. Since all of these FODMAPs contribute to similar symptoms, the effects of eating FODMAPs are cumulative; the more FODMAPs you eat, the greater your digestive woes. But have no fear—when writing the *Low-FODMAP 28-Day Plan: A Healthy Cookbook with Gut-Friendly Recipes for IBS Relief,* we carefully came up with a meal plan that minimizes FODMAPs in all of the recipes. This scientifically proven diet is rich in nutrition and variety—not to mention taste, especially with all the wonderful recipes we have put together for you.

Get ready to say good-bye to your digestive troubles and hello to delicious, comforting foods that truly nourish you. You will find this book to be a wonderful guide in learning how to incorporate the low-FODMAP diet into your life, how to identify your personal trigger foods, and how to prepare delicious meals that feed your body without hurting your belly. I am confident that you will find relief with the low-FODMAP eating plan.

Here's to a calmer belly and getting your life back.

Kate Scarlata, RDN, LDN
Registered and licensed dietitian specializing in digestive health and low-FODMAP diets
Bestselling author of The Complete Idiot's Guide to Eating Well with IBS.

Introduction

If you, a loved one, or someone you care for are among the 25 to 45 million Americans suffering from irritable bowel syndrome (IBS), then your daily food choices probably cause more than physical symptoms. Flare-ups of the condition can trigger feelings of anxiety, embarrassment, and isolation, too. Even worse, finding adequate medical treatments is often challenging and expensive.

Fortunately, the *Low-FODMAP 28-Day Plan* offers a way out of this suffering. More than just a recipe book, it contains all of the tools you need to regain some control over the condition and free yourself from the physical and emotional distress caused by IBS.

Why Low-FODMAP?

FODMAP is an acronym for "fermentable oligosaccharides, disaccharides, monosaccharides, and polyols." In simple terms, a low-FODMAP diet restricts certain types of carbohydrates, providing symptomatic relief for many people with IBS. By minimizing your consumption of foods containing FODMAPs, you significantly reduce your chances of experiencing unpleasant symptoms like bloating, cramps, and diarrhea.

You might feel intimidated by a diet that restricts the foods you are allowed to eat. Many aspects of family, social, and cultural life center around food, and by limiting your diet, it may seem as though you are limiting your lifestyle. The good news is that eating a low-FODMAP diet doesn't mean consuming bland, mushy foods. This book contains 105 delicious and enjoyable low-FODMAP recipes that appeal to the palate without disrupting the gut. In addition, it provides the following tools to help you achieve a low-FODMAP lifestyle that is both sustainable and enjoyable:

- Lists of high- and low-FODMAP ingredients that show what you can and cannot consume safely

- Detailed information about low-FODMAP diets to help you understand the hows and whys of the lifestyle

- In-depth meal plans for four weeks of delicious breakfasts, lunches, dinners, and snacks

- Prepared shopping lists for each week's meals to help you navigate the grocery store and stock your pantry

- Step-by-step recipes that make food preparation simple and easy

- Tips, tricks, and substitutions to help you customize the plan to your personal taste

With so many tasty dishes to choose from, your daily food choices will soon be driven by delicious flavors, not problem reactions. Get ready to enjoy a satisfying and symptom-free lifestyle.

PART ONE
Getting Started

What Is the Low-FODMAP Diet?

For many Americans, the word *diet* has negative connotations, drawing to mind a period of temporary deprivation and hard work in pursuit of weight loss. The low-FODMAP lifestyle isn't your typical diet experience, however. Instead, it is a customizable eating plan created to allow IBS sufferers like you or your loved one to make positive dietary changes, ensuring a more healthy future.

If you have IBS, then you already know the discomfort it can cause, with painful and embarrassing gastrointestinal symptoms including gas, cramping, bloating, and diarrhea. You may also be suffering from a reduced quality of life, because making plans can be difficult when you never know whether you will experience symptoms that require you to stay close to home. The low-FODMAP diet offers you the ability to live your life as you did before you had IBS: free from gastrointestinal discomfort and embarrassment. It is a positive lifestyle change that allows you to reduce your symptoms and improve your quality of life.

Why Follow a Low-FODMAP Diet?

In the 2000s, two researchers at Monash University in Australia, Peter R. Gibson and Susan J. Shepherd, set out to explore the relationship between food intake and symptoms in patients with IBS. What they discovered was an approach to eating that offered significant symptomatic relief in 75 percent of the people in the study. By making the same strategic changes in your diet, you may be able to experience a similar reduction in or elimination of the discomfort associated with IBS.

The Monash University studies have found that eliminating certain types of carbohydrates from the diet provided relief of IBS symptoms. They called these carbohydrates FODMAPs, which stands for fermentable oligosaccharides, disaccharides, monosaccharides, and polyols.

While all FODMAPs are carbohydrates, not all carbohydrates contain FODMAPs. The Digestive Health Center at the Stanford University Medical Center notes that there are certain types of carbohydrates in this category that you must avoid on a low-FODMAP diet:

- Fructose
- Lactose
- Fructans, also called inulin
- Galacto-oligosaccharides, also called GOS
- Polyols

Since most foods don't list these terms on nutritional labels, it's important to understand which foods and ingredients fall into the preceding categories. The following table shows prominent examples of each. All of the foods listed in the table must be eliminated from your diet during the initial four-week phase of the low-FODMAP diet if you want to experience maximum relief from your symptoms.

What to Expect with a Low-FODMAP Diet

Over the next four weeks, you will eliminate or minimize foods containing FODMAPs. During that time, you will track your IBS symptoms so you can note improvements and determine how the plan is working for you.

After four weeks, you will strategically reintroduce foods into your diet to determine which ingredients trigger your IBS symptoms. By identifying food triggers, you can begin to customize your low-FODMAP diet plan to meet your own unique needs.

Low-FODMAP Diet Guidelines

The key to relief of your symptoms is strictly following a low-FODMAP eating plan. Whenever you eat foods that contain FODMAPs, you may notice a return of unpleasant symptoms. The following guidelines can help you make the transition to low-FODMAP eating.

FODMAP Type	Common FODMAP Sources
Monosaccharides (fructose)	High-fructose corn syrup (HFCS), honey, agave nectar, apples, pears, mangos, asparagus, cherries, watermelon, fruit juice, sugar snap peas
Disaccharides (lactose)	Cow's milk, sheep's milk, goat's milk, ice cream, yogurt, sour cream, heavy cream, soft cheeses (such as ricotta and cottage cheese)
Oligosaccharides (fructans)	Onions, garlic, leeks, shallots, wheat, couscous, graham flour, pasta, rye, persimmons, watermelon, chicory, dandelion greens, artichokes, beets, asparagus, red cabbage, okra, radicchio, Brussels sprouts
Oligosaccharides (GOS)	Non-canned lentils, non-canned chickpeas (garbanzo beans), hummus, kidney beans, pinto beans, peas, whole soybeans
Polyols	Xylitol, mannitol, sorbitol, glycerol, isomalt, lactitol, maltitol, apples, apricots, peaches, nectarines, pears, plums, prunes, cherries, avocados, blackberries, lychees, cauliflower, mushrooms

- **Talk to your doctor.** Whenever you embark on a new eating plan, it is essential you meet with your primary health care provider. Talk to your doctor about getting screened for celiac disease before making plans to begin a low-FODMAP diet, since lowering your gluten intake with a low-FODMAP diet can make celiac testing inaccurate. If you have other serious food restrictions or health issues, such as a vegan diet or diabetes, it is especially important to seek medical advice before starting a low-FODMAP diet.

- **Follow the low-FODMAP diet strictly for four weeks, and track your progress.** Let your symptoms be your guide. Track your progress using the symptom tracker on page 12. If after four weeks you still aren't feeling better, continue for two more. If your symptoms persist after six weeks of strict adherence to a low-FODMAP diet, it is time to talk to your physician and engage in a new strategy for symptom management.

While early studies showed the effectiveness of a low-FODMAP diet for IBS, research is now underway to test how low-FODMAP eating may affect these other bowel health issues:

- Inflammatory bowel disease (IBD)
- Fructose intolerance
- Celiac disease
- Gluten intolerance

IBD

According to the Mayo Clinic, inflammatory bowel disease is an autoimmune condition involving inflammation of the digestive tract. The most common forms of IBD are Crohn's disease and ulcerative colitis. The University of Virginia Medical Center notes that while more research is needed, primary results indicate that a low-FODMAP diet may also help manage symptoms associated with IBD.

Fructose Malabsorption

Fructose malabsorption is a condition in which the body poorly tolerates fructose intake. Researchers at the University of Austria found that fructose malabsorption may cause symptoms similar to those of IBS. Since the low-FODMAP diet is also low in fructose, it may be effective in minimizing symptoms associated with fructose intolerance. However, while the low-FODMAP diet is low in fructose, it is not fructose-free, so it is best to discuss this plan with your primary health care provider before adopting it to manage fructose malabsorption.

Celiac Disease and Gluten Intolerance

Celiac disease is an inflammatory autoimmune disorder in which consumption of any foods containing gluten causes damage to the villi in the small intestine. This causes a number of attendant issues, including gastrointestinal distress and an inability to digest foods and absorb nutrients. Celiac disease is the most severe form of gluten intolerance. According to the National Foundation for Celiac Awareness, about 1 in 133 Americans has celiac disease.

The only treatment for celiac disease is a completely gluten-free diet. The low-FODMAP diet is not completely gluten-free, but it can easily be adapted to be so. Because of this, it may be helpful in management of celiac symptoms. However, some low-FODMAP diets include a few gluten-containing ingredients such as oats (which is often processed in the same factories as wheat and barley) and asafetida powder, which is often used as a replacement for onions. Avoid these ingredients if you choose a low-FODMAP diet to manage celiac disease.

- **After four to six weeks, begin reintroducing foods.** After following the diet strictly for four to six weeks, you will slowly add FODMAP-containing foods back into your diet in small amounts to determine which foods trigger your IBS symptoms.

  Reintroduce foods one at a time, and only in a small amount. During this time, track your symptoms to determine which foods are your own personal triggers. Note the food you've tried, the amount, and any symptoms you experienced as a result.

  To reintroduce foods:

1. Select a food that contains **only one** type of FODMAP from one of the groups (fructans, polyols, fructose, lactose, or GOS) you have eliminated. Avoid choosing foods like apples, which contain multiple FODMAPs. Otherwise, you won't know which FODMAP is triggering your symptoms.

2. Try a small amount of that food. For example, if you've really missed wheat, try $\frac{1}{2}$ cup of pasta at lunch or dinner and note any symptoms that occur within the next 24 hours.

3. If you experience symptoms, chances are that food group is a trigger. For example, if you had $\frac{1}{2}$ cup of pasta and you noticed symptoms, then fructans are likely to be a trigger. You will need to restrict them.

4. After your symptoms disappear, you can try a smaller amount of the same food or move on to another food group.

5. If you don't experience symptoms, try the same food or a similar food from the same group in a slightly larger quantity. For example, you may wish to have 1 cup of pasta or two slices of bread.

6. Again, track your symptoms for 24 hours. If you remain symptom-free, you may continue to try the same FODMAP group, adding slightly larger quantities each day. If, after a week, you still haven't had symptoms, then you can assume this group is not a trigger and move on to the next.

The entire reintroduction process can take as long as five or six weeks. Once complete, you will be able to customize the FODMAP diet to avoid your own personal triggers.

- **Read labels carefully.** Food manufacturers sneak all kinds of ingredients into processed foods. Therefore, it's up to you to learn the label terms that indicate when a food contains ingredients that may cause a flare-up of your IBS. See page 24 for food additives to avoid.

- **Eat unprocessed or minimally processed foods.** Because ingredients' labels can be so tricky to navigate, one of the best ways to avoid accidentally ingesting something that causes a flare-up is to eat as many whole, unprocessed foods as possible. The more a food has been altered from its natural state, the more likely it is to contain ingredients that may cause you difficulty. For example, a whole tomato used to make spaghetti sauce is far less likely to contain ingredients that cause issues than spaghetti sauce from a jar. Select unprocessed foods (normally found around the perimeter of the grocery store), including animal protein, suitable low-FODMAP fruits and vegetables, nuts and seeds (excluding pistachios and cashews), and lactose-free dairy.

- **Make foods from scratch whenever possible.** When you make your own food, you know exactly what goes into it. That isn't the case with processed foods, fast foods, and restaurant meals. If time is an issue, you can make several meals on the weekend and freeze or refrigerate them to have on hand all week. You can also double recipes so you will have leftovers for a second meal.

- **Plan meals and snacks.** Careful planning can help you avoid accidentally eating foods that contain FODMAPs. Plan meals and snacks a week in advance and compile a grocery list so you get all you need for the week in a single trip to the store. If you're traveling, take low-FODMAP foods with you.

- **Be prepared when dining out.** If you are planning to eat at a restaurant, familiarize yourself with the menu items that will fit within your low-FODMAP lifestyle before you go out to eat. Many restaurants list menus and nutrition information on their websites. In fine dining establishments, tell your waiter your dietary requirements so he or she can talk to the chef or suggest menu items that will suit your needs. See page 231 for more tips about dining out.

How to Identify Trigger Foods

Trigger foods are those that cause flare-ups of your symptoms, and people with IBS may have different trigger foods. You will most likely identify trigger foods once you have completed your initial four weeks of low-FODMAP eating and have begun reintroducing foods into your diet. If you are not strictly following the low-FODMAP plan before you begin reintroducing foods, then you will not be able to assess your triggers accurately.

The low-FODMAP diet is a dynamic process. Even after you've gone through the full elimination and reintroduction, you may encounter other foods that trigger your IBS. When you experience a flare-up of symptoms, use the following tips to identify the food or beverage that has triggered them.

- Track the foods you eat daily, even after the elimination and reintroduction phase of the diet.

- If you experience symptoms, check the foods you've eaten within eight hours of the start of symptoms. Look for unusual foods you haven't eaten before or you don't eat regularly.

- Avoid all of those foods for one week.

- Once symptoms have subsided, reintroduce the potential trigger foods in small amounts, one at a time.

- Note which of these foods trigger a recurrence of symptoms and remove them from your diet.

SYMPTOM TRACKER

Before beginning the low-FODMAP diet, record your baseline symptoms (gas, constipation, diarrhea, bloating, abdominal pain, etc.) and their severity on a scale of 1 to 10, where 1 is no reaction.

Symptom	Severity

Follow the low-FODMAP diet for four to six weeks. Record your symptoms at the end of each week to track your progress.

Time Period	Symptoms	Severity
End of week 1		
End of week 2		
End of week 3		
End of week 4		
End of week 5		
End of week 6		

If your symptoms have improved dramatically, you can reintroduce foods containing FODMAPs back into your diet one at a time. Use the following table to track your body's reactions to each FODMAP food type.

FODMAP Type	Food and Serving Size	Date/Time of Eating	Symptoms	Conclusion

Foods to Enjoy and Avoid

To help you make sense of which foods contain FODMAPs and which do not, the following table shows foods you need to eliminate and foods you can enjoy on a low-FODMAP diet. For foods that must be consumed in moderation, recommended serving sizes have been included.

Foods to Eliminate (High-FODMAP)	Foods to Enjoy (Low-FODMAP)	Foods to Enjoy in Moderation (Moderate-FODMAP)
FRUITS		
apples, apricots, avocados, blackberries, boysenberries, cherries, figs, fruit juice, lychees, mangos, nectarines, pears, persimmons, plums, prunes, watermelon	bananas, blueberries, cantaloupe ($3/4$ cup), clementines, cranberries, grapes, honeydew ($3/4$ cup), kiwis, lemons, limes, oranges, passion fruit, pineapples, raspberries, rhubarb, star fruit, strawberries	avocados (1 tablespoon), banana chips (10 chips), shredded coconut ($1/4$ cup), dried cranberries (1 tablespoon), grapefruit, pomegranate (1 small pomegranate or $1/4$ cup), raisins (1 tablespoon)
VEGETABLES		
asparagus, artichokes, beets, cauliflower, chicory, corn, garlic, scallions (white part), leeks (white part), mushrooms, okra, onions, peas, shallots, sugar snap peas	alfalfa sprouts, bean sprouts, bell peppers, bok choy, carrots, chiles, cucumbers, eggplant, endive, fennel, green beans, kale, leeks (green part), lettuce, olives, parsnips, potatoes, scallions (green part), spinach, summer squash, Swiss chard, turnips, zucchini	artichoke hearts ($1/8$ cup), broccoli ($1/2$ cup), Brussels sprouts, butternut squash ($1/4$ cup), celery (5-inch stalk), green cabbage (1 cup), radicchio (1 cup), savoy cabbage ($1/2$ cup), sweet potatoes ($1/2$ cup), tomato (1 tomato per meal)

continued

Foods to Eliminate (High-FODMAP)	Foods to Enjoy (Low-FODMAP)	Foods to Enjoy in Moderation (Moderate-FODMAP)

STARCHES AND LEGUMES

barley, couscous, hummus, kidney beans, lima beans, pinto beans, rye, soybeans, wheat (and wheat-containing products, such as bread, cereal, crackers, flour, pasta, pretzels, tortillas, etc.)	arrowroot, gluten-free cornbread and corn tortillas, gluten-free breads, gluten-free flour, gluten-free pasta, millet, quinoa, rice, tapioca, tofu, tempeh	Buckwheat kernels ($1/8$ cup), canned chickpeas ($1/4$ cup), gluten-free oats ($1/4$ cup dry or $1/2$ cup cooked), canned lentils ($1/4$ cup), sourdough spelt bread (2 slices)

DAIRY

buttermilk, cottage cheese, custard, ice cream, milk (cow, goat, sheep), pudding, sour cream, most soy milks, yogurt	butter, coconut milk, lactose-free cow's milk, rice milk, whipped cream ($1/2$ cup)	Brie cheese, feta cheese, mozzarella cheese, hard cheeses (such as Parmesan, cheddar, and Swiss) (1 ounce); half-and-half ($1/4$ cup); soft cheeses (such as ricotta and cream cheese) (2 tablespoons)

NUTS AND SEEDS

cashews, pistachios	Brazil nuts, chia seeds, macadamia nuts, peanuts, peanut butter, pecans, pine nuts, sesame seeds, sunflower seeds, walnuts	almonds (10 nuts), flaxseed (1 tablespoon), hazelnuts (10 nuts)

MEATS

processed meats containing wheat, garlic, onion, or HFCS	beef, chicken, duck, eggs, fish, game meats, lamb, pork, seafood, tofu, turkey	

Foods to Enjoy and Avoid

Foods to Eliminate (High-FODMAP)	Foods to Enjoy (Low-FODMAP)	Foods to Enjoy in Moderation (Moderate-FODMAP)
CONDIMENTS		
condiments containing wheat, garlic, onion, or HFCS (such as barbecue sauce, ketchup, mayonnaise, mustard, teriyaki sauce, tomato paste)	champagne vinegar, fish sauce, garlic-infused oil (recipe on page 220), lemon juice, lime juice, oils, oyster sauce, red wine vinegar, rice vinegar, sherry vinegar, gluten-free soy sauce (tamari), white wine vinegar	balsamic vinegar (1 tablespoon)
HERBS AND SPICES		
garlic powder or salt, onion powder or salt	basil, bay leaves, caraway, cayenne, chervil, chives, cilantro, coriander, dill, ginger, mint, mustard seed, oregano, paprika, parsley, pepper, red pepper flakes, rosemary, salt, thyme, turmeric	allspice (1 teaspoon), cinnamon (1 teaspoon), onion-free and garlic-free chili powder (1 teaspoon), cumin (1 teaspoon)
SWEETENERS		
agave, agave nectar, agave syrup, HFCS, honey, isomalt, mannitol, sorbitol, xylitol	acesulfame-potassium (acesulfame-k), aspartame, brown sugar, pure maple syrup (2 tablespoons), sucrose, granulated sugar, powdered sugar	

Food Allergies versus Food Intolerances

Some people use the terms "food allergies" and "food intolerances" interchangeably. Medically, however, there is a difference between the two.

According to the Mayo Clinic, the difference between allergies and intolerances lies in how your body reacts when you consume the offending food.

Food allergies cause an immediate immune system response in your body whenever you consume the item to which you are allergic. This immune response can affect many of your body's different organs, and symptoms are often quite severe. This occurs when you consume even a tiny amount of the offending food, so you must avoid all foods to which you are allergic. Allergic reactions may include:

- Anaphylaxis (inflammation and closing of breathing passages)
- Upper respiratory symptoms
- Swelling or tingling of mouth, face, lips, throat, and tongue
- Watery eyes
- Sudden onset of diarrhea, vomiting, or cramps
- Skin reactions such as hives
- Drop in blood pressure
- Difficulty breathing

Food intolerances are much slower acting than allergies. Symptoms do not result from an immune system reaction. Instead, they typically come on gradually or may occur only when you eat a significant amount of the offending food. For example, in some cases, IBS results from FODMAP intolerances. Intolerances often manifest as gastrointestinal distress, although some may trigger asthma or other respiratory symptoms.

FODMAP FAQs

You've been given a lot of information, and you probably have questions. That's completely normal. The following are the most commonly asked questions about low-FODMAP diets.

1. How will I know if the low-FODMAP diet will work for me?

If you have IBS, studies have shown the diet is effective in about 75 percent of cases where people have strictly adhered to the dietary guidelines. Research is less clear about the diet's efficacy in cases of other bowel disorders, including IBD and celiac disease. After discussing it with your doctor, the best way to know for certain whether the diet will work for you is to try it. When you do, track your symptoms, and follow the guidelines exactly. If, after six weeks, you continue to have symptoms, the diet may not be right for you.

2. Will I ever be able to go back to eating bread (or some other food I love)?

Maybe. While there's a good chance you'll have to follow some type of FODMAP restriction for the rest of your life, different people have varying FODMAP triggers. During the reintroduction phase, you'll discover these triggers. Foods that trigger symptoms will need to be avoided for a few months at least. But since tolerances to FODMAPs can change over time, you can try to reintroduce your favorite foods in small amounts again later to see if your tolerances have improved.

3. Can I enjoy a glass of wine, a beer, or a mixed drink on the low-FODMAP diet?

WebMD notes that alcoholic beverages can trigger IBS symptoms. While most alcoholic beverages aren't high in FODMAPs, they can irritate your condition. You should be able to determine whether alcohol is one of your personal triggers by tracking symptoms. You may want to do this outside of your initial low-FODMAP diet and reintroduction of food so you don't confuse your results or misidentify a trigger.

4. What about coffee, tea, and soda?

Black coffee doesn't contain FODMAPs, and black, green, and peppermint teas are low in FODMAPs. However, other teas like chamomile and oolong do contain FODMAPs, and sodas often have HFCS. Caffeine can stimulate bowel movements, which may be a problem for some people. When it comes to beverages, proceed with caution.

5. Is a low-FODMAP diet gluten-free?

Wheat, barley, and rye are primary sources of gluten, and the diet restricts these. Some gluten-containing ingredients are allowed on the low-FODMAP diet, however. In a gluten-free diet for celiac disease, it is essential to avoid any wheat, barley, and rye and to avoid cross-contamination of these ingredients. Unless you also have celiac disease or some other form of gluten intolerance, it isn't necessary to be as strict about cross-contamination in a low-FODMAP diet as it is in a gluten-free diet for celiac disease. If you have celiac disease, you can make the low-FODMAP diet completely gluten-free, but you must also avoid any foods that contain traces of gluten, as well as cross-contamination.

6. Can I cheat?

It is important to follow the plan strictly until you begin to reintroduce foods after the initial four weeks.

7. How can I get flavor into my food without using garlic and onions?

There are several strategies you can use to flavor your foods. To replace onion and garlic flavor you can:

- Use the green part of scallions or leeks (but not the white part).
- Use a pinch of asafetida powder. If you have celiac disease, then you'll need to choose asafetida powder that is gluten-free.
- Make garlic oil by simmering garlic in oil and then removing all traces of the solid garlic (see page 220).
- Make onion oil by simmering onions in oil and then removing all traces of the solid onion (see page 220).

8. Can I adapt a low-FODMAP diet to a paleo/low-carb/low-calorie/low-fat diet?

Yes, the low-FODMAP diet can be adapted to any eating plan. However, it is essential you talk with your doctor and/or work with a dietitian to ensure you are receiving proper nutrition.

9. I have diabetes. Can I be on a low-FODMAP diet?

You can, although you will need to do a lot of adapting of the diet to meet your own dietary needs. One of the groups of foods restricted on the low-FODMAP diet is sugar alcohols, which are commonly used in sweet treats for diabetics. Before trying the low-FODMAP diet, talk with the health care provider and the dietitian managing your diabetes care.

10. Will I get all the nutrients I need on a low-FODMAP diet?

The low-FODMAP diet can be a balanced diet depending on the foods you choose. For example, if you choose to eat only potato chips and candy bars to avoid FODMAPs, then the diet won't be balanced. However, if you choose foods from all food groups, then chances are you will get the nutrients you need. You can also work with a dietitian or physician to ensure you are eating a fully balanced and healthy diet.

2

How to Use the Meal Plan

The chapters that follow contain a detailed meal plan to help you make the most of your first four weeks on the low-FODMAP diet. The meal plan is specially designed to make the diet as fail-safe as possible, keeping you on track for the full four weeks. The meal-planning chapters discuss potential pitfalls you may encounter each week and also provide helpful tips to keep you motivated.

Along with four weeks' worth of detailed daily meal plans, including breakfast, lunch, dinner, and two snacks, you'll also find extensive shopping lists. These lists are based on the meals and snacks recommended in the weekly plans. Using the shopping lists can help you save time and money while reducing waste.

Finally, you'll discover time-saving tips to help you fit the four-week meal plan into your busy schedule. Tips include items you can make ahead of time on the weekends so you can stay on track throughout the week, as well as instructions for storing premade foods appropriately for use later in the week.

Getting the Most out of Your Meal Plan

Careful planning is one of the best ways to ensure success in any diet. With that in mind, this cookbook provides you with the tools you need to succeed.

Before getting started, it's also essential to set yourself up for success. Before jumping into the low-FODMAP diet, you'll need to prepare your home to create a no-fail environment.

General Tips

The following general tips can help you prepare:

- **Talk to your family about the low-FODMAP diet.** Tell them why you will be following it. Explain that improving your quality of life will also improve their quality of life, and ask for their support in your efforts. Ask that they not tempt you with off-plan foods, and that they offer support when you're eating out together.

- **Empty out your pantry, cupboard, and refrigerator of all high-FODMAP foods.** To create a no-fail environment, it's essential to remove any foods that might tempt you to cheat.

- **Plan your schedule.** Because you will be cooking most of your food and avoiding processed and fast foods, you'll need to plan extra time for shopping and cooking.

- **Sit down with the meal plan ahead of time and make sure you are familiar with the recipes.** If you substitute recipes in the meal plan with other recipes in this book, alter the shopping list with the appropriate ingredients so you don't wind up with extra food that might go to waste.

If you have celiac disease or need to avoid gluten, then you will also need to clean kitchen surfaces to remove potential gluten contamination. Clean out utensil drawers and cupboards that may contain bread crumbs or other traces of food. One source of cross-contamination many people forget about is the knife block, which often harbors bread crumbs. Clean it thoroughly. Keep utensils used for gluten-free cooking in a separate area. Store gluten-free snacks and flours on upper shelves to prevent contamination by crumbs or dust from gluten-filled products.

Shopping Tips

The following tips can make your trips to the grocery store more productive and budget-friendly:

- **Leave plenty of time for grocery shopping.** It will take longer than usual, because you will be reading labels carefully at the store.

- **Find a low-FODMAP tool that works for you.** Some low-FODMAP tools are listed on page 236.

- **Know which ingredients you should buy organic and which you can purchase conventional.** The Environmental Working Group has created a list of the "Dirty Dozen" and "Clean Fifteen" produce items (page 234). The Dirty Dozen foods are very high in pesticides. Whenever possible, purchase organic versions of these foods. Dirty Dozen foods that are low-FODMAP include cherry tomatoes, cucumbers, grapes, hot peppers, potatoes, spinach, strawberries, sweet bell peppers, kale, and zucchini. The Clean Fifteen foods are low in pesticides. Therefore, you can purchase conventionally grown versions of these foods. Members of the Clean Fifteen that are low-FODMAP include green cabbage, cantaloupe, eggplant, grapefruit, kiwis, and pineapples.

Reading Food Labels

As mentioned previously, you'll be spending more time reading food labels in the grocery store, looking for ingredients that are high in FODMAPs. Read the ingredients even for foods called for in the recipes in this cookbook, because some brands may contain high-FODMAP additives or ingredients.

Stock Your Pantry

A well-stocked pantry is the key to your success. Fill yours with low-FODMAP foods you will use in your cooking, as well as with snacks you can enjoy between meals. With a well-stocked pantry and refrigerator, it's easier to remain on track throughout your four-week eating plan. The foods in the following list are essential to many recipes in this book.

Refrigerator

Having the following foods on hand will help you prepare low-FODMAP foods for meals:

- **Lactose-Free Milk**   Dairy products containing lactose can aggravate IBS symptoms. Many lactose-free dairy products, which use enzymes to break down milk sugars, are commonly available. If you are sensitive to dairy, you can also enjoy rice milk, which is naturally lactose-free. Many of the breakfast and dessert recipes in this book call for lactose-free milk.

• **Lactose-Free Plain Yogurt** This yogurt has been prepared with enzymes that break down lactose. Choose plain yogurt instead of flavored because it is less likely to have high-fructose corn syrup (HFCS) in it. Lactose-free plain yogurt is used in a number of breakfast and dessert recipes in this book. In a pinch, you can also use it as a replacement for sour cream.

High-FODMAP Food Additives

When reading labels, look for the following ingredients, which may aggravate your IBS. While the following list is far from comprehensive, avoid foods that contain the following ingredients:

- High-fructose corn syrup (HFCS)
- Corn syrup
- Corn sugar
- Honey
- Agave nectar
- Fruit juice
- Any ingredient that contains the word "wheat"
- Any ingredient that contains the word "rye"
- Any ingredient that contains the word "barley" (except barley malt vinegar or barley malt flavoring)
- Semolina
- Flour
- Fructose
- Sweeteners ending in -ol
- Herb and spice blends (may contain onion or garlic)
- Artificial flavorings
- Inulin
- Flours made from legumes

- **Cheddar Cheese**   This hard cheese is relatively low in lactose, so it won't irritate IBS. It's great for snacking, or for a quick gluten-free cheese sandwich. It's used in some of the lunch and dinner recipes in this cookbook. Limit yourself to 1 ounce per serving.

- **Unsalted Butter**   Low in lactose, unsalted butter is used in a number of the dessert and breakfast recipes in this book.

- **Eggs**   Eggs are a staple of low-FODMAP living. They are high in protein, and used in many of the breakfast, lunch, and dessert recipes in this book. Hard-boiled eggs make a great low-FODMAP snack or salad ingredient.

- **Extra-Firm Tofu**   If you are a vegetarian or vegan, extra-firm tofu is an essential element of low-FODMAP cooking because it provides necessary protein. Tofu is used in a few of the vegetarian dinners in this book.

- **Chia Seeds**   These tiny black seeds offer protein, fiber, and omega-3 fatty acids. When you combine them with liquid and allow them to sit for about 10 minutes, they form a viscous gel that works for thickening smoothies and puddings.

Freezer

Keep the following items in your freezer for your low-FODMAP lifestyle:

- **Gluten-Free Sandwich Bread**   Keep an extra loaf of gluten-free sandwich bread in the freezer so you'll always have something low-FODMAP to snack on. Choose bread that doesn't have high-fructose corn syrup (HFCS) or similar ingredients, such as Udi's gluten-free white sandwich bread, which tastes great. Many of the breakfast and lunch recipes call for gluten-free sandwich bread.

- **Frozen Berries**   Select IQF (individually quick frozen) unsweetened blueberries, raspberries, or strawberries. They work well for a quick smoothie or dessert topping.

- **Homemade Vegetable Stock**   Use the recipe on page 99 to make your own homemade vegetable stock. Freeze it in 2- to 4-cup containers so you can easily prepare soups or stews without having to make the stock each time.

- **Herbs in Olive Oil**   Many of the recipes in this book call for chopped fresh herbs. When you have fresh herbs left over, chop them and mix 1 tablespoon of the chopped herbs with 1 tablespoon of olive oil. Freeze in ice cube trays, and then transfer the ice cubes to labeled zipper-top plastic bags. That way, you'll always have fresh herbs to add quick flavor to a meal or snack.

- **Frozen Shrimp**   Frozen cooked shrimp can be thawed quickly in cold water and used to make a simple, satisfying meal. It can be a time-saving substitute for raw shrimp in many of the dinner and lunch recipes in this book.

- **Vegetable Trimmings**   As you make your low-FODMAP foods, don't throw away vegetable trimmings. Instead, store them in a zipper-top plastic bag in the freezer. You can then use them when you're making vegetable stock.

Meat

Having the following meat products on hand can help keep you on plan:

- **Bacon**   Bacon is low-FODMAP, easy to cook, and very satisfying. Even a small amount adds a ton of flavor to many of the soups, stews, and salads in this book.

- **Plain Deli-Sliced Meats**   Choose plain thin-sliced deli meats instead of those flavored with honey, garlic, or Italian seasonings, and keep them in the refrigerator. They're great on a cracker, for a quick sandwich, or wrapped around a slice of melon. You can also use them to replace cooked meats in many of the salads in this cookbook. Remember to check the label if you need to avoid gluten, since some deli meats are not gluten-free.

- **Boneless, Skinless Chicken Breast**   Chicken breast with the bones and skin removed is easy to turn into a quick low-FODMAP meal. It's also a great way to add protein to the salads in this book.

- **Lean Ground Beef**   You can cook ground beef in so many ways that it's the perfect meat to keep around for a quick but flavorful meal, including several of the soups and dinners in this book. Choose beef with 15 percent fat or less.

Produce

Having plenty of low-FODMAP fruits and vegetables on hand provides you with foods for a quick snack or allows you to cook a healthy meal.

- **Lettuce**   Keep a variety of lettuce types in the crisper drawer of the refrigerator. Lettuce is a great sandwich topping, and it's easy to whip up as a salad on the go.

- **Scallions**   Also known as green onions or spring onions, the green part of scallions can add onion flavor to soups, stews, and main dishes without FODMAPs. Be sure to remove the white part of the scallion entirely, which can cause IBS flare-ups. Many of the recipes in this book call for scallion greens.

- **Cantaloupe and Honeydew**   These two melons make a great breakfast, side dish, or snack. They're also tasty in smoothies and desserts and are featured in many of the dessert recipes in this book. Stick to ¾ cup or less when eating either of these melons.

- **Lemons and Limes**   Freshly squeezed lemon and lime juice, as well as grated lemon and lime zest, can add flavor and brightness to many low-FODMAP dishes, including salads, vinaigrettes, sauces, and soups. Many of the recipes contained in this book call for lemon or lime juice.

- **Dark, Leafy Greens**   Spinach, kale, and Swiss chard are all nutritional powerhouses that are loaded with antioxidants. They can be blended in smoothies, steamed, sautéed, or eaten in soups, sandwiches, and salads.

- **Ginger**   Fresh ginger can be minced or grated into many of the soup and dessert recipes you'll find in this cookbook for added flavor and brightness.

Spice Rack

Spices add flavor to foods, so it's essential to keep them on hand:

- **Bay Leaves**   These flat green leaves can be simmered in soups and sauces to add flavor. Be sure to remove the bay leaves before serving.

- **Sea Salt**   Sea salt is more flavorful than table salt, but it is also less refined. Virtually every savory dish in this book calls for sea salt.

- **Peppercorns**   Peppercorns come in many different colors, including green, pink, white, and black. Black peppercorns are the most commonly used in savory recipes to add flavor. Instead of buying preground black pepper, grind your own peppercorns for the best flavor.

- **Dried Herbs**   A number of dried herbs are available to add flavor to dishes. Stock your pantry with some of the more commonly used herbs such as thyme, basil, rosemary, and sage, which are used in many of the soup and main dish recipes in this book. Avoid herb blends since they may contain onion or garlic.

- **Dried Spices**   Spices come from ground seeds and bark. They can add tremendous flavor to foods. You'll want to keep on hand cinnamon, nutmeg, allspice, cumin, and coriander, which are used in desserts, soups, and breakfasts throughout this book.

Pantry

The pantry is where you'll store many of your low-FODMAP foods for cooking:

- **Gluten-Free All-Purpose Flour**   This flour typically substitutes cup for cup for wheat flour in several desserts. Choose a brand that doesn't use flour made from legumes.

- **Gluten-Free Baking Mix (homemade or Bisquick)**   While you can make your own Gluten-Free Baking Mix (page 201), Gluten-Free Bisquick Baking Mix makes it very easy to prepare baked goods such as biscuits, pancakes, and waffles. It's a handy substitute for several dessert and breakfast recipes in this book.

- **Nuts and Seeds**   A handful of low-FODMAP nuts and seeds are perfect for a quick snack, and they're used in many snack recipes in this book. Stock your pantry with peanuts, peanut butter, walnuts, pecans, macadamia nuts, sunflower seeds, and pumpkin seeds. If you want to try something a little different, try chia seeds. Chia seeds are packed with fiber, omega fatty acids, and antioxidants, and they are well-tolerated by people who need to follow a low-FODMAP diet.

- **Rice**   Brown and white rice are both low in FODMAPs. Keep plenty in the pantry for an easy side dish, or for use in soups and stews.

- **Gluten-Free Pasta**   Some gluten-free pasta is made with legume flours, so read labels carefully. Choose pasta made with low-FODMAP flours such as rice, quinoa, and corn. Many of the main dishes in this book call for gluten-free pasta.

Essential Equipment

You'll be doing a lot of cooking, so you'll need the right equipment to help make it easier. Using the right equipment can help save time and effort in the kitchen.

Cooking Utensils

The following cooking utensils will make it easier to prepare low-FODMAP recipes:

- **Chef's Knife**   You'll be chopping a lot of vegetables in the weeks to come, so you'll want a good, sharp chef's knife. A chef's knife has a long blade and comfortable handle that allows you to rock the knife as you chop quickly.

- **Parchment Paper**   You can find parchment paper alongside the foil at the grocery store. This paper is heatproof and used to line pans to create a nonstick surface.

- **Pepper Grinder**   Freshly ground black pepper is much more flavorful than preground pepper, so a pepper grinder is a must for most kitchens.

- **Rubber Scraper**   A rubber scraper allows you to fully scrape ingredients from pans, mixing bowls, blenders, and food processors. If you choose a heatproof rubber scraper, you'll also be able to use it to stir hot items when you cook them.

- **Slotted Spoon**   A slotted spoon allows you to remove solids from liquids without losing any of the liquid. Choose one with a long, heatproof handle.

- **Spatula**   Choose a flat spatula with an angled head, which will help you flip pancakes, cook eggs, and perform many other tasks. Silicone is heatproof, and it won't harm nonstick surfaces.

- **Tongs**   Tongs are helpful in grilling and sautéing. Select tongs with a long handle and heatproof grips.

- **Whisk**   Many sauces and egg dishes call for whisking, because the wires on a whisk help incorporate air. Choose a whisk with a comfortable, nonslip handle that is easy to grip.

- **Wooden Spoons**   You'll need an assortment of large wooden spoons for stirring, baking, and cooking. Choose wooden spoons in a natural finish.

Appliances

Kitchen gadgets make cooking easier and quicker. The recipes in this cookbook call for a number of appliances:

- **Blender** Use a blender to make smoothies, blend sauces and soups, and mix batters. Choose a blender that has several speeds.

- **Food Processor** Food processors chop, puree, and mix. In this cookbook, the food processor is used for making mayonnaise and other sauces.

- **Mixer** You can use either a hand mixer or a stand mixer, preferably with whisk and beater attachments. These are used to whip eggs for many of the dishes in this book.

- **Slow Cooker** Put ingredients in your slow cooker in the morning and then come home to a hot meal. Many of the recipes in this book can be adapted to slow cooker use.

Pots and Pans

You'll also need a few pots and pans to make your job easier:

- **9-by-13-Inch Baking Pans** These versatile baking pans are ideal for everything from roasting meat to baking casseroles.

- **Baking Sheets** Use these shallow metal pans for baking cookies, toasting bread, and many other tasks.

- **Oven-Safe 12-Inch Skillet** Use this round, flat skillet for sautéing meat and making stir-fries, and for any tasks that involve going from the stove top to the oven. Select a stainless-steel or cast-iron skillet with an oven-safe handle.

- **12-Inch Nonstick Sauté Pan/Skillet** This round, flat skillet has a coating such as Teflon to keep meat and eggs from sticking. Use it for stir-fries, sautés, and many other tasks.

- **12-Quart Stockpot with Lid** A large stockpot is useful for cooking big batches of soups and stocks, including the vegetable stock in this book.

- **6-Quart Saucepan with Lid** A medium-sized saucepan can be used for smaller batches of soups and for steaming vegetables.

- **2-Quart Saucepan with Lid** Use a small saucepan for making puddings, reheating soups, and boiling water.

Tips and Tricks to Make Your Day Easier

With a busy life, taking shortcuts can help you save time. The following tips and tricks can help you stay on track with your new low-FODMAP lifestyle:

- **Whenever possible, use precooked meats.** This works especially well for salads and sandwiches, where cooking the meat in the same pan as the vegetables and other ingredients isn't essential for flavor development. For example, in most of the salad recipes you can start with cooked meat instead of cooking the raw meat yourself.

- **Choose prechopped and prewashed vegetables.** Use bagged salad, chopped salad bar veggies, and other supermarket shortcuts to save time and effort.

- **For weekday lunches and dinners, prepare as many ingredients ahead of time as possible**. Chop fruits, vegetables, and meats and store them in a tightly sealed container in the refrigerator. Boil eggs for salads on the weekends, and make vinaigrette ahead of time.

- **Use instant rice.** Regular rice takes 20 minutes or longer to cook. Instant rice is ready in 5 minutes. You can also purchase precooked rice in the freezer or rice section of the supermarket.

- **Parcook pasta.** Cook pasta to 75 percent done, and then run it under cold water to stop cooking. Toss it with a bit of olive oil and store it in a tightly sealed container in the refrigerator until you're ready to use it (up to one week). Then cook it for the remaining 25 percent of the time in boiling water to serve.

- **Make stock on weekends**. Many of the recipes in this book call for vegetable stock. You can double or triple the recipe to make a large pot so you only have to make it once or twice over the four weeks of the diet. Store it in 2- to 4-cup servings in the freezer and thaw as necessary.

3

The Low-FODMAP Diet Meal Plan in Action

This chapter is your launch pad for starting the low-FODMAP diet! In this chapter, you'll find weekly meal plans, pantry and shopping lists, and prep-ahead recommendations to reduce the amount of time you spend in the kitchen on weeknights. The menus cover three meals for each day, and offer a list of snacks you can choose from. Be sure to enjoy one or two snacks between meals each day to avoid getting so hungry that you are tempted to make bad choices.

Enjoying meals is an important part of living to the fullest, so give yourself the time and space to adjust to this new way of eating.

Week One

You're ready to begin your first week of low-FODMAP cooking and dining. Soon, you'll begin to feel better than you have in a long time. This chapter has all the tools you need to be successful as you begin your journey to better health.

During this first week, it is essential you monitor your symptoms using the symptom tracker on page 13. While most people experience immediate relief within the first seven days, it may take much longer before you see the full effect. Be patient as the low-FODMAP diet helps your colon begin to heal.

The first week is essentially a "detox" week where your body rids itself of all of the FODMAPs you've been eating until now, so you may notice some cravings for foods you cannot have. This may be especially true for wheat. According to Mark Hyman, who is a physician, author, and chair of the Institute for Functional Medicine, wheat is addictive because it has compounds that act on opioid receptors in the brain. The addiction will begin to fade after three to five wheat-free days. In the meantime, cravings are normal and to be expected.

To fight wheat and other cravings, plan to have a few low-FODMAP snacks and treats available. If you get a particularly intense craving, try engaging in an activity that releases endorphins into the brain, such as 10 minutes of exercise or meditation. The endorphins will help calm your food craving.

Week One Menu at a Glance

Your first week of meals includes breakfast, lunch, dinner with dessert, an afternoon snack, and an evening snack. Feel free to move snacks around as needed. To minimize waste and save time, meals and snacks use similar ingredients. Lunch and dessert recipes can be eaten as leftovers within a day or two of preparing them. Recipes included in this book are indicated with an asterisk (*).

Day One

BREAKFAST Mixed Berry–Chia Breakfast Smoothie*

LUNCH Spinach, Strawberry, and Walnut Salad,* Balsamic Dijon Dressing*

AFTERNOON SNACK 2 rice cakes, 2 tablespoons almond butter

DINNER Steamed Clams,* rice, steamed vegetables, Lemon Squares*

EVENING SNACK Vanilla Chia Pudding with Blueberries*

Day Two

BREAKFAST Spiced Pumpkin Quinoa and Oat Cereal*

LUNCH Asian Ginger Chicken and Rice Soup*

AFTERNOON SNACK 2 cups Spiced Popcorn*

DINNER Gluten-Free Penne with Basil-Walnut Pesto,* lettuce and tomato salad, Balsamic Dijon Dressing,* Lemon Squares*

EVENING SNACK 2 cups Spiced Popcorn*

Day Three

BREAKFAST 2 hard-boiled eggs, 3/4 cup honeydew melon

LUNCH deli rotisserie chicken on a bed of lettuce, Balsamic Dijon Dressing*

AFTERNOON SNACK 1 (5-inch) celery stalk, 1 tablespoon almond butter, 1 tablespoon raisins

DINNER Maple-Soy Glazed Salmon,* sautéed spinach, Lemon-Rosemary Granita*

EVENING SNACK 1 ounce cheddar cheese, 2 rice cakes

Day Four

....

BREAKFAST crisp rice cereal, $\frac{1}{2}$ sliced banana, $\frac{1}{2}$ cup rice milk

LUNCH Asian Ginger Chicken and Rice Soup,* $\frac{1}{2}$ sliced banana

AFTERNOON SNACK $\frac{3}{4}$ cup honeydew melon cubes

DINNER Chicken Piccata,* lettuce and tomato salad, Balsamic Dijon Dressing,* Lemon-Rosemary Granita*

EVENING SNACK 1 ounce Baked Corn Tortilla Chips,* $\frac{1}{2}$ cup Baba Ghanoush*

Day Five

....

BREAKFAST $\frac{1}{2}$ cup lactose-free plain yogurt, $\frac{1}{2}$ cup halved grapes

LUNCH Deli rotisserie chicken, 1 cup rice, $\frac{3}{4}$ cup honeydew melon

AFTERNOON SNACK 10 baby carrots, 1 tablespoon almond butter or 2 tablespoons peanut butter

DINNER hamburger patties on toasted gluten-free buns, Low-FODMAP Mayonnaise,* lettuce and tomato salad, Balsamic Dijon Dressing,* Butterscotch Pudding*

EVENING SNACK 1 ounce Baked Corn Tortilla Chips,* $\frac{1}{2}$ cup Baba Ghanoush*

Day Six

....

BREAKFAST Potato and Kale Frittata*

LUNCH Lettuce Wrap with Shrimp Salad,* sliced kiwi

AFTERNOON SNACK $\frac{1}{2}$ cup halved grapes, 1 ounce peanuts

DINNER Halibut with Lemon-Basil Beurre Blanc and Braised Endive,* Butterscotch Pudding*

EVENING SNACK 2 Deviled Eggs,* $\frac{1}{2}$ cup halved grapes

Day Seven

....

BREAKFAST Poached Eggs on Red Potato Hash*

LUNCH Stuffed Baked Potato with Broccoli and Cheddar*

AFTERNOON SNACK 1 slice gluten-free toast, 2 tablespoons peanut butter

DINNER Filet Mignon with Red Wine Pan Sauce,* smashed red potatoes, steamed zucchini, Berry Summer Pudding*

EVENING SNACK 2 Deviled Eggs,* 1 wedge honeydew melon

Pantry List

Grains
Cereal, gluten-free/HFCS-free
    (such as Rice Krispies)
Crackers, gluten-free/HFCS-free
Popcorn kernels (not microwavable)
Quick oats, gluten-free
Rice cakes
White rice

Oil/Vinegar/Condiments
Balsamic vinegar
Canola oil
Champagne vinegar
Dijon mustard
Olive oil
Red wine vinegar
Soy sauce, gluten-free
White vinegar
Worcestershire sauce

Baking
All-purpose flour, gluten-free
Baking powder, gluten-free
Baking soda
Brown sugar, light
Brown sugar, dark
Cornstarch
Gluten-free baking mix
    (such as Bisquick)
Granulated sugar
Maple syrup, pure
Table salt
Vanilla extract, pure

Nuts/Seeds
Chia seeds
Peanut butter
Peanuts
Pecans
Sunflower seeds
Walnuts

Dried Herbs/Spices/Seasonings
Allspice
Basil
Bay leaves
Black peppercorns
Cayenne pepper
Chili powder
Chinese five-spice powder
Cinnamon
Cumin
Italian herbs
Nutmeg
Oregano
Paprika
Sea salt
Star anise
Tarragon
Thyme

Canned/Jarred
Pumpkin puree, unsweetened
    (15 ounces)
Capers (3.5 ounces)

Grocery List

Dairy

Butter, unsalted (1 pound)

Cheese, cheddar (8 ounces)

Eggs, large (2 dozen)

Half-and-half (1 pint)

Rice milk ($\frac{1}{2}$ gallon)

Whole milk, lactose-free ($\frac{1}{2}$ gallon)

Yogurt, plain, lactose-free (8 ounces)

Meat/Seafood

Beef, lean ground (1 pound)

Beef, tenderloin steaks
   (four 4-ounce steaks)

Chicken, boneless, skinless breasts
   (2 pounds)

Chicken, rotisserie (1)

Clams, in shells (4 pounds)

Halibut (fillets, 1 pound)

Salmon (fillets, 1 pound)

Shrimp, cooked ($\frac{1}{2}$ pound)

Other

Dry red wine (1 bottle)

Dry white wine (1 bottle)

Raisins (1 box)

Sandwich bread, gluten-free
   (2 loaves)

Fruit

Banana (1)

Blueberries (1 pint)

Golden raspberries (1 pint)

Grapes (1 pound)

Honeydew melon (1)

Kiwi (1)

Lemons (14)

Oranges (7)

Raspberries (2 pints)

Strawberries (3 pints)

Leafy Greens

Belgian endive (4 heads)

Kale (1 bunch)

Lettuce, butter (1 head)

Lettuce, iceberg (1 head)

Lettuce, romaine (2 heads)

Spinach (1 pound)

Vegetables

Bell peppers, red (4)

Bok choy (1 head)

Broccoli (1 pound)

Carrots (6)

Carrots, baby (1 pound)

Celery (1 package)

Eggplant (1)

Scallions (3 bunches)

Potatoes, red (1 pound)

Potatoes, russet (1)

Tomatoes, beefsteak (4)

Zucchini (1 pound)

Fresh Herbs

Basil (1 bunch)

Chives (1 bunch)

Garlic (1 bulb) ➤

Ginger (1-inch knob)

Parsley, flat-leaf (1 bunch)

Rosemary (1 bunch)

Tarragon (1 bunch)

Thyme (1 bunch)

You can make a few substitutions to this list if you have food allergies or sensitivities:

- If you are allergic to shrimp or other shellfish, replace the shrimp with shredded chicken from the deli rotisserie chicken.

- For dairy allergies, replace half-and-half with rice milk.

- To keep wine fresh longer, you can buy four-packs of small bottles and just use one at a time.

Prep Ahead for Week One

Scratch cooking can be time-consuming and frustrate you when you are embracing a new diet. Cooking during the week goes much more quickly if you prep as many ingredients as possible ahead. Do your prep on Saturday or Sunday to get a good start on your week of food. It will prepare you psychologically for the challenge ahead, thus helping you stay on track over the long term.

- Prepare a double recipe of Garlic Oil (page 220) for use during the week. Store in a tightly sealed container in the refrigerator.

- Make the Balsamic Dijon Dressing (page 222) and store in a tightly sealed container in the refrigerator. Whisk or shake well before using.

- Prepare 5 cups of cooked white rice and freeze in 1-cup servings in zipper-top plastic bags. Thaw in the microwave for use.

- Bake the Lemon Squares (page 206). Cover with plastic wrap and refrigerate.

- Make a double recipe of homemade Vegetable Stock (page 99). Store in five 2-cup servings, tightly sealed, in the refrigerator or freezer. If frozen, thaw on the stove top before using.

- Portion the deli rotisserie chicken into five servings, removing skin and bones. Store in zipper-top plastic bags or sealed containers for use in lunches.

- Hard-boil 6 eggs. Store in the refrigerator, unpeeled, until ready to use.

- Cube the melon and portion into several $3/4$-cup servings. Refrigerate in individually sealed bags or containers.

- Cook the penne pasta and store in a tightly sealed container in the refrigerator. Reheat in the microwave.

Week Two

Congratulations on making it through your first week of low-FODMAP living. You may be starting to notice a change in your symptoms by now. These differences may be small, or they may be quite noticeable. During the second week, you will continue with your low-FODMAP diet plan, eating the healthy foods found in this cookbook, as well as other healthy meals and snacks.

This week, it is likely you will notice fewer cravings for foods you used to eat, such as wheat. While some detoxification may continue to occur, if you do notice cravings, they will most likely be milder and of briefer duration. Continue to engage in the strategies listed in the previous chapter for overcoming cravings.

If, however, you find yourself struggling to stick with this diet, don't worry. It's normal to experience difficulties when following a new diet. To help yourself stay motivated, remind yourself of the value in what you are doing. Your struggle is temporary, while the eventual relief you will receive from your symptoms can bring about changes that last a lifetime. This is a good week to ask for encouragement from friends and family. Explain to them the goals of low-FODMAP eating and ask them to help you follow the diet so you can feel better.

Give yourself plenty of TLC this week. Reward yourself for sticking to your eating plan with a special treat such as a massage or a manicure. You can use other strategies to help uplift your spirit as well, such as meditation, yoga, or light exercise.

Week Two Menu at a Glance

The meal plans this week continue to include breakfast, lunch, dinner, and two snacks. Feel free to substitute any recommended meals with others in this book that may better suit your personal tastes or schedule. Recipes included in this book are indicated with an asterisk (*).

Day One

BREAKFAST Banana-Spinach Green Smoothie*

LUNCH Spicy Egg Salad Sandwich*

AFTERNOON SNACK Baked Garlic Oil Potato Chips*

DINNER African Peanut Soup*

EVENING SNACK 2 hard-boiled eggs

Day Two

BREAKFAST Berry, Macadamia Nut, and Yogurt Breakfast Parfaits*

LUNCH Cobb Salad*

AFTERNOON SNACK 1 slice gluten-free toast, 2 tablespoons peanut butter

DINNER Shrimp Scampi,* gluten-free angel hair pasta, Mixed Berry Yogurt Ice Pop*

EVENING SNACK 1 ounce Baked Corn Tortilla Chips,* Crab Rangoon Dip*

Day Three

BREAKFAST 2 scrambled eggs, 1 slice gluten-free toast with butter, ¼ cup sliced strawberries

LUNCH Pasta Salad with Ham and Vegetables*

AFTERNOON SNACK Baked Garlic Oil Potato Chips*

DINNER Easy Beefaroni,* steamed vegetables, Mixed Berry Yogurt Ice Pop*

EVENING SNACK 1 ounce cheddar, gluten-free crackers ➤

Day Four

BREAKFAST gluten-free cereal, $\frac{1}{2}$ sliced banana, $\frac{1}{2}$ cup rice milk or lactose-free milk

LUNCH Ground Beef and Cabbage Soup*

AFTERNOON SNACK $\frac{1}{2}$ banana, $\frac{1}{2}$ cup plain lactose-free yogurt

DINNER Slow-Cooker Turkey Porcupine Meatballs,* steamed vegetables, Lime Curd with Meringue Topping*

EVENING SNACK 1 ounce Baked Corn Tortilla Chips,* $\frac{1}{4}$ cup Fresh Salsa*

Day Five

BREAKFAST $\frac{1}{2}$ cup plain lactose-free yogurt, $\frac{1}{2}$ cup sliced strawberries, 1 slice gluten-free toast with butter

LUNCH Ground Beef and Cabbage Soup*

AFTERNOON SNACK 1 (5-inch) celery stalk, 2 tablespoons peanut butter

DINNER Teriyaki Chicken,* rice, steamed broccoli, 2 Peanut Butter Cookies*

EVENING SNACK $\frac{1}{2}$ cup sliced strawberries

Day Six

BREAKFAST Huevos Rancheros*

LUNCH Open-Face Bacon, Tomato, and Cheddar Sandwich,* $\frac{1}{2}$ orange

AFTERNOON SNACK $\frac{1}{2}$ orange, 1 ounce peanuts

DINNER Minted Lamb Chops,* roasted red potatoes, steamed vegetables, Crêpes with Blueberry Filling*

EVENING SNACK 2 Peanut Butter Cookies,* $\frac{1}{2}$ cup lactose-free milk

Day Seven

BREAKFAST Orange-Vanilla French Toast*

LUNCH Monte Cristo Sandwich,* lettuce and tomato salad, oil and vinegar

AFTERNOON SNACK Cheese Quesadilla,* $\frac{1}{4}$ cup Fresh Salsa*

DINNER Grilled Shrimp Tacos with Cilantro,* Strawberry Shortcake*

EVENING SNACK 2 rice cakes, 2 tablespoons peanut butter

Pantry List

Grains
Cereal, gluten-free/HFCS-free
Crackers, gluten-free/HFCS-free
Rice cakes
White rice

Oil/Vinegar/Condiments
Dijon mustard
Horseradish
Hot pepper sauce
Olive oil
Red wine vinegar
Soy sauce, gluten-free
Worcestershire sauce

Dried Herbs/Spices/Seasonings
Allspice
Basil
Bay leaves
Black peppercorns
Cayenne pepper
Cinnamon
Coriander
Cumin
Sea salt
Thyme

Baking
Baking powder, gluten-free
Brown sugar, dark
Gluten-free baking mix
Maple syrup, pure
Potato starch
Rice flour

Nuts/Seeds
Peanut butter
Peanuts
Sesame seeds

Canned/Jarred
Artichoke hearts (4.5 ounces)
Coconut milk (15 ounces)
Jalapeño peppers, chopped (4 ounces)
Olives, black (8 ounces)
Tomatoes, crushed
    (two 15-ounce cans)
Tomatoes, diced (14.5 ounces)
Tomato sauce, onion-free/garlic-free
    (8 ounces)

Grocery List

Dairy and Eggs
Butter, unsalted (1 pound)
Cheese, blue (4 ounces)
Cheese, cheddar (16 ounces)

Cheese, cream (4 ounces)
Cheese, mozzarella (4 ounces)
Cheese, Swiss (4 ounces)
Eggs, large (3 dozen) ➤

Rice milk ($\frac{1}{2}$ gallon)

Whole milk, lactose-free ($\frac{1}{2}$ gallon)

Yogurt, plain, lactose-free
    (two 32-ounce containers)

Meat/Seafood

Beef, lean ground (3 pounds)

Chicken, boneless, skinless
    breasts (20 ounces)

Crabmeat, lump (8 ounces)

Ham, baked (1 pound)

Ham, deli-sliced (12 ounces)

Lamb, loin chops
    (four 4- to 5-ounce chops)

Shrimp, jumbo, raw ($2\frac{1}{2}$ pounds)

Turkey, ground ($1\frac{1}{2}$ pounds)

Other

Corn tortillas, 6-inch (24)

Dry white wine (1 bottle)

Elbow macaroni, gluten-free
    (1 pound)

Rotini, gluten-free (1 pound)

Spaghetti, gluten-free (9 ounces)

Wooden skewers

Fruit

Bananas (2)

Blueberries (2 pints)

Kiwi (1)

Honeydew melon ($\frac{1}{2}$ melon)

Lemon (1)

Limes (8)

Oranges (2)

Raspberries (1 pint)

Strawberries (4 pints)

Leafy Greens

Cabbage, green (1 head)

Lettuce, iceberg (2 heads)

Lettuce, romaine (2 heads)

Spinach, baby (9-ounce bag)

Vegetables

Bell peppers, green (1)

Bell peppers, red (1)

Broccoli (1 pound)

Carrots (8)

Celery (2 bunches)

Scallions (4 bunches)

Jalapeño peppers (1)

Potatoes, red (1 pound)

Potatoes, russet (4)

Potatoes, sweet (2)

Tomatoes, cherry (1 pint)

Tomatoes, heirloom or beefsteak (2)

Tomatoes, Roma (10)

Fresh Herbs

Basil (1 bunch)

Chives (2 bunches)

Cilantro (2 bunches)

Garlic (1 bulb)

Ginger (1-inch knob)

Mint (1 bunch)

Parsley, curly (1 bunch)

Parsley, flat-leaf (1 bunch)

Thyme (1 bunch)

Prep Ahead for Week Two

Prepping as many ingredients as possible ahead of time will help you stay on track. Cooking from scratch at the end of a busy day is much faster if you have already prepared and stored some of the staple ingredients. Take some time over the weekend to get a good start. It will help you focus on the job at hand, ensuring that the week ahead will be a dieting success.

- Grill the chicken for the Cobb Salad, and store in a tightly sealed container in the refrigerator.

- Make the Cobb Salad dressing (page 92), and store in a tightly sealed container in the refrigerator.

- Hard-boil the eggs for egg salad and snacks.

- Cut up the vegetables for salads and soups, and store in tightly sealed containers in the refrigerator.

- Cook the pasta, and store in a tightly sealed container in the refrigerator.

- Make the Vegetable Stock (page 99) for both soups.

- Cook the bacon for sandwiches, and store in a zipper-top plastic bag in the refrigerator.

- Grate the cheese and portion it out for meals. Store in tightly sealed containers in the refrigerator.

- If using your own Gluten-Free Baking Mix (page 201), mix it up and store in a tightly sealed container at room temperature.

- Make the Baked Corn Tortilla Chips (page 118), and store in a tightly sealed container at room temperature.

- Make the Fresh Salsa (page 128), and store in a tightly sealed container in the refrigerator.

Week Three

It's week three, and things should be getting a little easier for you now. There's a good chance you've noticed a significant change in your IBS symptoms. Keep it up, and soon you'll notice higher energy levels and a more positive outlook, too.

If you're feeling better this week, you may notice the urge to sneak a few high-FODMAP foods. This is a normal response but not advisable. You've come a long way in the past two weeks, and it's important to allow your gut to heal by continuing to eat low-FODMAP foods.

If you feel the urge to cheat this week, try the following strategies:

- Review your symptom tracker (page 12) and note how much better you're feeling. Once you start feeling better, it's easy to forget how bad you felt before.

- Seek support from friends and family.

- Find a delicious, low-FODMAP treat that feels like you're cheating. Have a little bit when you feel the urge to cheat.

- When you feel the urge to sneak a high-FODMAP food, wait 10 minutes. Cravings typically fade within that period.

- If you're still feeling the urge to cheat after waiting 10 minutes, distract yourself—take a warm bath, meditate, exercise, spend time with a loved one, or go for a walk. All of these can help reset you and keep you on track.

Week Three Menu at a Glance

You can substitute other meals in this cookbook for any below that you don't want. Recipes included in this book are indicated with an asterisk (*).

Day One

BREAKFAST Ham, Egg, and Swiss Crustless Quiche*

LUNCH Greek Salad with Mint and Cucumber*

AFTERNOON SNACK 1 ounce Sweet 'n' Spicy Pecans*

DINNER Sweet and Sour Tofu,* rice, strawberries

EVENING SNACK 1 ounce Baked Corn Tortilla Chips,* ½ cup Baba Ghanoush*

Day Two

BREAKFAST Ham, Egg, and Swiss Crustless Quiche*

LUNCH Chicken and Spicy Sprout Wrap,* ½ banana

AFTERNOON SNACK ½ banana, 1 ounce peanuts

DINNER Meatloaf "Muffins,"* steamed spinach, mashed potatoes,
      Honeydew-Mint Sorbet*

EVENING SNACK 1 ounce Sweet 'n' Spicy Pecans*

Day Three

BREAKFAST Low-FODMAP Pancakes with Strawberry Topping*

LUNCH Vegetable Soup with Ground Pork and Macaroni*

AFTERNOON SNACK 2 rice cakes, 2 tablespoons peanut butter

DINNER Chicken Carbonara,* lettuce and tomato salad, oil and vinegar,
      Honeydew-Mint Sorbet*

EVENING SNACK 1 ounce Baked Corn Tortilla Chips,* ½ cup Baba Ghanoush*   ➤

Day Four

BREAKFAST Cereal, ½ sliced banana, ½ cup rice milk or lactose-free milk

LUNCH Vegetable Soup with Ground Pork and Macaroni*

AFTERNOON SNACK 1 (5-inch) celery stalk, 2 tablespoons peanut butter

DINNER Grill-Poached Halibut with Lemon and Dill,* grilled zucchini, Maple-Glazed Grilled Pineapple*

EVENING SNACK 2 wedges honeydew melon wrapped with 2 thin slices ham

Day Five

BREAKFAST Maple-Pecan Breakfast Quinoa*

LUNCH Arugula Salad with Feta, Olives, and Heirloom Tomatoes*

AFTERNOON SNACK 1 ounce cheddar cheese, gluten-free crackers

DINNER Chicken Fingers,* baby carrots, oven fries, Lemon Meringue Shells with Raspberries*

EVENING SNACK 1 slice gluten-free toast, 2 tablespoons peanut butter

Day Six

BREAKFAST 2 scrambled eggs, Low-FODMAP Breakfast Sausage*

LUNCH Tuna Melt,* 1 orange

AFTERNOON SNACK 1 wedge honeydew melon

DINNER Thin-Cut Pork Chops with Mustard-Chive Pan Sauce,* steamed broccoli, baked potato, Lemon Meringue Shells with Raspberries*

EVENING SNACK 1 ounce Sweet 'n' Spicy Pecans*

Day Seven

BREAKFAST Eggs Benedict*

LUNCH Salade Niçoise*

AFTERNOON SNACK 1 slice gluten-free bread with 1 ounce melted cheddar cheese

DINNER Slow-Cooker Pulled Pork Sandwiches with Ginger Slaw,* Orange-Almond Dutch Baby*

EVENING SNACK 2 rice cakes, 2 tablespoons peanut butter

Pantry List

Grains
Cereal, gluten-free/HFCS-free
Crackers, gluten-free/HFCS-free
Quinoa
Rice cakes
White rice

Oil/Vinegar/Condiments
Canola oil
Dijon mustard
Horseradish
Olive oil
Rice vinegar
Soy sauce, gluten-free
White vinegar

Baking
All-purpose flour, gluten-free
Almond flavoring
Baking powder, gluten-free
Cornstarch
Cream of tartar
Gluten-free baking mix
Maple syrup, pure
Powdered sugar

Nuts/Seeds
Peanut butter
Pecan halves (16 ounces)

Dried Herbs/Spices/Seasonings
Allspice
Bay leaves
Black peppercorns
Cayenne pepper
Cinnamon
Cumin
Italian herbs
Liquid smoke
Marjoram
Oregano
Red pepper flakes
Rosemary
Sage, ground
Sea salt
Smoked paprika

Canned/Jarred
Black olives (8 ounces)
Green olives (8 ounces)
Pineapple, in juice (6 ounces)
Tomatoes, fire-roasted (8 ounces)
Tuna, water-packed (20 ounces)

Grocery List

Dairy and Eggs

Butter, unsalted (1 pound)
Cheese, cheddar (8 ounces)
Cheese, cream (4 ounces)
Cheese, feta (4 ounces)
Cheese, mozzarella (4 ounces)
Cheese, parmesan (4 ounces)
Cheese, Swiss (4 ounces)
Eggs, large (3 dozen)
Rice milk ($\frac{1}{2}$ gallon)
Tofu, extra-firm (14 ounces)
Whole milk, lactose-free ($\frac{1}{2}$ gallon)

Meat/Seafood

Bacon (8 slices)
Beef, lean ground ($1\frac{1}{2}$ pounds)
Canadian bacon (4 thick slices)
Chicken, boneless, skinless breasts
   (3 pounds)
Chicken, deli-sliced (12 ounces)
Halibut (one 16-ounce fillet)
Ham, baked (1 pound)
Pork, thin-cut chops
   (eight 2-ounce chops)
Pork, ground (2 pounds)
Pork, boneless shoulder (3 pounds)

Other

Corn tortillas (6-inch) (24)
Dry white wine (1 bottle)

Elbow macaroni, gluten-free
   (1 pound)
Hamburger buns, gluten-free (6)
Niçoise olives (8 ounces)
Sandwich bread, gluten free (1 loaf)
Spaghetti, gluten-free (1 pound)

Fruit

Banana (1)
Lemons (15)
Honeydew melon (2)
Oranges (5)
Pineapple (1)
Raspberries (1 pint)
Strawberries, frozen (8 ounces)
Strawberries, fresh (1 pint)

Leafy Greens

Arugula, 9 ounces
Cabbage, green (1 head)
Lettuce, butter (1 head)
Lettuce, iceberg (1 head)

Vegetables

Baby carrots (1 pound)
Bell peppers, green (2)
Bell peppers, yellow (1)
Broccoli (1 pound)
Carrots (6)
Celery (10 stalks)

Cucumber (1)

Eggplant (1)

Fennel (1 bulb)

Green beans (12 ounces)

Scallions (4 bunches)

Potatoes, baby red (8)

Potatoes, russet (8)

Sprouts, spicy (1 container)

Tomatoes, cherry (2 pints)

Tomato, heirloom or beefsteak (1)

Zucchini (3)

Fresh Herbs

Basil (1 bunch)

Chives (1 bunch)

Dill (1 bunch)

Garlic (1 bulb)

Ginger (1-inch knob)

Mint (3 bunches)

Parsley (1 bunch)

Thyme (1 bunch)

Niçoise olives can typically be found at the salad bar in the grocery store. If you can't find them, you can substitute any other olives of your choosing.

Prep Ahead for Week Three

If you've got a busy week, you can prep the following ingredients and recipes ahead of time.

- Prepare the Vegetable Stock (page 99) for soups, and store in a tightly sealed container in the refrigerator or freezer.

- Boil 6 eggs and store, unpeeled, in the refrigerator.

- If using your own Gluten-Free Baking Mix (page 201), mix it up and store in a tightly sealed container at room temperature.

- Prepare the Baba Ghanoush (page 119), and store in a tightly sealed container in the refrigerator.

- Prepare and cook the Low-FODMAP Breakfast Sausage (page 72), and store in a tightly sealed container in the refrigerator.

- Prepare vinaigrette for salads and store in a tightly sealed container in the refrigerator. Whisk or shake well before using.

- Make the Baked Corn Tortilla Chips (page 118), and store in a tightly sealed container at room temperature.

- Prepare the Sweet 'n' Spicy Pecans (page 127), and store in a tightly sealed container at room temperature.

- Make the Ranch Dressing (page 226), and store in a tightly sealed container in the refrigerator.

Week Four

Congratulations for getting this far. At last, you've reached the final week of your strict elimination diet. To keep your symptoms at bay, it's important to go full steam ahead. Starting next week you will reintroduce foods in a slow and controlled manner, so this week you need to stay on track so you don't inadvertently cause a recurrence of symptoms.

Chances are you're feeling much better. As symptoms fade, the urge to slip in a few high-FODMAP favorites may be stronger now. You've come a long way, and you are almost done with the toughest part. It's important to keep your gut healthy so you know which foods cause your symptoms when you begin reintroducing them next week. If you try to sneak in a few high-FODMAP foods before this time, you may not get accurate results, which may cause you to eliminate foods from your diet that don't cause symptoms. After all the hard work over the past three weeks, it is worth staying focused for just seven more days.

Focus on ending the four weeks of your diet on a strong note. That way, you'll be as symptom-free as possible when you begin reintroducing FODMAPs one at a time next week. If you feel discouraged this week or experience the urge to cheat, look at how far you've come and remind yourself that you have only one week to go. Utilize the strategies you've learned over the past few weeks to stick with this final week. Tell yourself, or ask others to remind you, that the toughest part is behind you now. After this week is over, you'll learn what you can eat and what you need to limit or eliminate for lifelong management of your IBS.

Week Four Menu at a Glance

This last week of menus will carry you through the home stretch of the elimination phase of the low-FODMAP diet. Foods with an asterisk (*) are recipes you can find in this cookbook.

Day One
....
BREAKFAST Mixed Berry–Chia Breakfast Smoothie*

LUNCH Chef Salad with Turkey, Ham, and Ranch Dressing*

AFTERNOON SNACK Baked Corn Tortilla Chips,* ¼ cup Fresh Salsa*

DINNER Lentil and Vegetable Sloppy Joes,* Baked Garlic Oil Potato Chips,*
   Oat Crumble with Rhubarb Sauce*

EVENING SNACK 2 hard-boiled eggs

Day Two
....
BREAKFAST 2 scrambled eggs with chopped green peppers

LUNCH Chicken Salad with Grapes*

AFTERNOON SNACK 2 rice cakes, 2 tablespoons peanut butter

DINNER Easy Lamb Stew,* Oat Crumble with Rhubarb Sauce*

EVENING SNACK Baked Corn Tortilla Chips,* 1 ounce cheddar cheese,
   ¼ cup Fresh Salsa*

Day Three
....
BREAKFAST Berry, Macadamia Nut, and Yogurt Breakfast Parfait*

LUNCH Soup of vegetables cooked in Vegetable Stock,* 1 slice gluten-free toast

AFTERNOON SNACK Popcorn with butter

DINNER Hearty Clam Chowder with Fennel,* 2 Peanut Butter Cookies*

EVENING SNACK Mixed Berry Yogurt Ice Pop*

Day Four

BREAKFAST cereal, ½ sliced banana, ½ cup rice milk or lactose-free milk

LUNCH Ham and Peppers Chopped Salad*

AFTERNOON SNACK Baked Garlic Oil Potato Chips*

DINNER Steak Fajitas with Peppers,* ¼ cup Fresh Salsa,* Mixed Berry
Yogurt Ice Pop*

EVENING SNACK Ham, cheese, gluten-free crackers

Day Five

BREAKFAST Gluten-free oatmeal with ½ cup blueberries

LUNCH Grilled cheese sandwich on gluten-free sandwich bread, baby carrots

AFTERNOON SNACK 2 Peanut Butter Cookies,* ½ cup lactose-free milk

DINNER Scallops with White Wine Tarragon Sauce,* steamed spinach, rice,
Crêpes with Blueberry Filling*

EVENING SNACK 1 slice gluten-free toast, 2 tablespoons peanut butter

Day Six

BREAKFAST Fried Eggs on Sautéed Spinach and Red Peppers*

LUNCH Chicken and Spicy Sprout Wrap,* sliced strawberries

AFTERNOON SNACK Cheese Quesadilla,* ¼ cup Fresh Salsa*

DINNER Lemon Pepper Cod with Braised Fennel,* Orange-Vanilla Smoothie*

EVENING SNACK 1 orange

Day Seven

BREAKFAST Orange-Vanilla French Toast*

LUNCH Monte Cristo Sandwich,* Baked Garlic Oil Potato Chips*

AFTERNOON SNACK Vanilla Chia Pudding with Blueberries*

DINNER Balsamic Dijon Grilled Chicken Skewers with Mixed Bell Peppers,*
baked potato, Maple-Glazed Grilled Pineapple*

EVENING SNACK 2 rice cakes, 2 tablespoons peanut butter

Pantry List

Grains
Cereal, gluten-free/HFCS-free
Crackers, gluten-free/HFCS-free
Oats, gluten-free
Popcorn kernels (not microwavable)
Rice cakes
White rice

Oil/Vinegar/Condiments
Balsamic vinegar
Canola oil
Dijon mustard
Olive oil
Red wine vinegar
Soy sauce, gluten-free
White vinegar
Worcestershire sauce

Dried Herbs/Spices/Seasonings
Bay leaves
Black peppercorns
Cayenne pepper
Cinnamon
Sea salt
Thyme

Baking
All-purpose flour, gluten-free
Almond flavoring
Baking powder, gluten-free
Brown sugar
Granulated sugar
Maple syrup, pure
Powdered sugar

Nuts/Seeds
Chia seeds
Macadamia nut pieces (1 cup)
Peanut butter
Peanuts
Walnuts

Canned/Jarred
Capers (3.5 ounces)
Lentils, canned (8 ounces)
Olives, black (8 ounces)
Tomatoes, crushed (14.5 ounces)
Tomato sauce (14.5 ounces)
Pepperoncini, sliced (4 ounces)

Grocery List

Dairy and Eggs
Butter, unsalted (1 pound)
Cheese, cheddar (8 ounces)
Cheese, cream (4 ounces)
Cheese, parmesan (4 ounces)
Cheese, Swiss (4 ounces)

Eggs, large (2 dozen)
Rice milk ($\frac{1}{2}$ gallon)
Whole milk, lactose-free ($\frac{1}{2}$ gallon)
Yogurt, plain, lactose-free
    (two 32-ounce containers)

Meat/Seafood

Bacon, pepper ($\frac{1}{2}$ pound)

Beef, flank steak (1 pound)

Chicken, boneless, skinless breasts
     (2 pounds)

Chicken, deli-sliced (12 ounces)

Cod (four 4-ounce fillets)

Ham, baked (12 ounces)

Ham, deli-sliced (18 ounces)

Lamb, ground (1 pound)

Sea scallops, large (16)

Turkey, deli-sliced (8 ounces)

Other

Corn tortillas (6-inch) (30)

Dry white wine (1 bottle)

Hamburger buns, gluten-free (4)

Sandwich bread, gluten-free
     (2 loaves)

Wooden skewers

Fruit

Banana (1)

Blueberries (2 pints)

Grapes ($\frac{1}{2}$ pound)

Lemons (4)

Limes (1)

Oranges (12)

Pineapple (1)

Raspberries (2 pints)

Rhubarb (1 pound)

Strawberries (2 pints)

Leafy Greens

Kale (1 pound)

Lettuce, butter (1 head)

Lettuce, romaine (2 heads)

Spinach, baby (9-ounce bag)

Vegetables

Bell peppers, green (5)

Bell peppers, red (7)

Bell peppers, orange (1)

Bell peppers, yellow (2)

Carrots (9)

Celery (7 stalks)

Cucumber (1)

Scallions (3 bunches)

Jalapeño peppers (1)

Leeks (2)

Potatoes, baby red (12)

Potatoes, russet (8)

Sprouts, spicy (1 container)

Tomatoes, heirloom or beefsteak (3)

Zucchini (1)

Fresh Herbs

Chives (2 bunches)

Cilantro (1 bunch)

Dill (1 bunch)

Garlic (1 bulb)

Parsley (1 bunch)

Tarragon (1 bunch)

Thyme (1 bunch)

If you can't find ground lamb for the lamb stew, you can replace it with an equal amount of lean ground beef.

Prep Ahead for Week Four

As always, prepping ahead on the weekend will save you time when you're in a hurry for the week. There are several items you can prep ahead this week.

- Prepare the Vegetable Stock (page 99), and store in a tightly sealed container in the refrigerator or freezer.

- Make the Baked Corn Tortilla Chips (page 118), and store them in a tightly sealed container at room temperature.

- Prepare the Baked Garlic Oil Potato Chips (page 122), and store them in a tightly sealed container at room temperature.

- Prepare the baked potatoes and store them, wrapped in foil, in the refrigerator. Reheat in the microwave.

- Hard-boil the eggs.

- Prepare the Low-FODMAP Mayonnaise (page 224), and store it in a tightly sealed container in the refrigerator.

- Bake the topping for the Oat Crumble with Rhubarb Sauce (page 203), and store in a tightly sealed container at room temperature.

PART TWO
Low-FODMAP Recipes

4

Breakfast

Mixed Berry–Chia Breakfast Smoothie

NUT-FREE   VEGETARIAN   VEGAN   PALEO-FRIENDLY   DAIRY-FREE   SOY-FREE

Prep time: 5 minutes   **Cook time:** None

Quick and easy for weekday mornings, this breakfast smoothie uses two types of berries. The smoothie is thickened with chia seeds, which also add protein. If fresh berries aren't available, you can use frozen berries instead, which will give the smoothie a thicker texture.

    2 cups unsweetened rice milk
    3 tablespoons chia seeds
    1 cup sliced strawberries
    1 cup raspberries
    2 tablespoons pure maple syrup

1. In a liquid measuring cup, stir together the rice milk and chia seeds. Set aside, allowing the chia seeds to soak in the milk until the mixture thickens, about 10 minutes.

2. Stir the seeds and milk once more. Scrape the mixture into a blender jar. Add the strawberries, raspberries, and maple syrup.

3. Blend the smoothie on high until it is well combined, about 2 minutes. Serve.

Serves 2 / **Per Serving**   Calories: 180   Protein: 4. 5 grams
Sugar: 19. 5 grams   Fat: 6. 65 grams

INGREDIENT VARIATIONS

If you'd like to boost the protein in this smoothie, add 1 or 2 egg whites before blending. For safety, use pasteurized eggs or farm-fresh eggs you've purchased within the past 2 days. Each egg white adds about 16 calories and 3. 6 grams of protein.

Banana-Spinach Green Smoothie

NUT-FREE VEGETARIAN VEGAN PALEO-FRIENDLY DAIRY-FREE SOY-FREE

Prep time: 5 minutes   **Cook time:** None

Green smoothies have gained popularity because of the nutrients, fiber, and antioxidants in dark, leafy greens. This smoothie uses spinach, which is high in vitamins A, C, and B$_6$. Spinach also contains magnesium and iron. If you prefer, you can replace the spinach with kale. For a sweeter smoothie, be sure to add the optional maple syrup.

    2 cups unsweetened rice milk
    2 cups baby spinach
    1 banana, peeled
    1 cup honeydew melon cubes
    $\frac{1}{2}$ teaspoon ground cinnamon
    1 tablespoon pure maple syrup (optional)

Place all of the ingredients in the jar of a blender. Blend on high speed until smooth, about 2 minutes. Serve.

Serves 2 / **Per Serving**   Calories: 235   Protein: 5. 5 grams
Sugar: 34. 5 grams   Fat: 3. 7 grams

TIME-SAVING TIP

To save time, you can blend the smoothie and keep it in the refrigerator for up to 3 days. That way, if you need breakfast on the go, you'll already have a smoothie ready.

Berry, Macadamia Nut, and Yogurt Breakfast Parfaits

VEGETARIAN   SOY-FREE

Prep time: 10 minutes   **Cook time:** None

Kids love these breakfast parfaits because they contain sweet berries and creamy yogurt. The recipe also contains macadamia nuts, which add protein and crunch.

    1 (32-ounce) container plain lactose-free yogurt
    4 cups sliced strawberries
    1 cup macadamia nut pieces

1. Dollop 2 spoonfuls of the yogurt into the bottoms of four dessert or parfait dishes.

2. Top with $\frac{1}{4}$ cup of the sliced strawberries.

3. Top with 1 tablespoon of the macadamia nut pieces.

4. Add 2 more spoonfuls of the yogurt.

5. Repeat steps 2 through 4 until you've layered all of the ingredients in each parfait glass, reserving some of the macadamia nut pieces for the garnish.

6. Finish with a sprinkling of macadamia nut pieces and serve immediately.

Serves 4 / **Per Serving**   Calories: 305   Protein: 15 grams
Sugar: 14 grams   Fat: 16 grams

Spiced Pumpkin Quinoa and Oat Cereal

VEGETARIAN   VEGAN   DAIRY-FREE   SOY-FREE

Prep time: 5 minutes   **Cook time:** 20 minutes

This spiced pumpkin cereal provides a warm start to the day. Oatmeal is high in fiber, while pumpkin provides vitamin A, vitamin C, and additional fiber. When serving, offer lactose-free milk and brown sugar for those wanting a creamier or sweeter cereal.

1 cup unsweetened pumpkin puree

4 cups water

Pinch salt

$3/4$ teaspoon ground cinnamon

1 cup quick oats

1 cup quinoa, rinsed

$1/2$ cup walnut pieces

1. In a large saucepan over medium-high heat, stir together the pumpkin, water, salt, and cinnamon and bring to a boil, stirring frequently. Add the oats and quinoa.

2. Reduce the heat to medium and cook, stirring frequently, until the oats and quinoa are cooked, about 15 minutes.

3. Remove from the heat and stir in the walnuts. Serve immediately.

Serves 4 / Per Serving   Calories: 278   Protein: 9 grams
Sugar: 6 grams   Fat: 11. 25 grams

WARNING

If your diet must remain strictly gluten-free, be sure to use oats that are certified gluten-free and have been processed in a facility that does not manufacture other gluten-containing foods.

Maple-Pecan Breakfast Quinoa

Prep time: 5 minutes   **Cook time:** 30 minutes

Many people think quinoa is just for dinner, but this recipe allows you to make a delicious breakfast quinoa with maple and cinnamon flavors. If you'd like to add a little sweetness, you can add $\frac{1}{4}$ cup raisins. Serve it topped with additional lactose-free milk and maple syrup, if you wish.

1 cup quinoa

2 cups lactose-free whole milk

2 cups water

$\frac{1}{2}$ cup pure maple syrup

Pinch salt

$\frac{1}{4}$ cup pecan pieces

$\frac{1}{4}$ teaspoon ground cinnamon

1. In a medium-sized saucepan over medium-high heat, stir together the quinoa, milk, water, maple syrup, and salt. Bring to a boil, stirring occasionally.

2. Reduce the heat to medium. Cover and simmer, stirring occasionally, until the quinoa softens, about 25 minutes.

3. Remove the quinoa from the heat and stir in the pecan pieces and cinnamon. Serve immediately.

Serves 4 / **Per Serving**   Calories: 298   Protein: 4 grams
Sugar: 26. 75 grams   Fat: 5. 2 grams

Orange-Vanilla French Toast

NUT-FREE   VEGETARIAN

Prep time: 5 minutes   **Cook time:** 10 minutes

French toast is a family favorite. This low-FODMAP French toast uses lactose-free milk in place of cream and gluten-free bread. Serve with maple syrup on the side, if desired.

2 cups lactose-free whole milk

6 large eggs

Juice and grated zest of 1 orange

1 teaspoon pure vanilla extract

8 slices gluten-free sandwich bread

2 tablespoons unsalted butter

Ground nutmeg, for garnish

1. In a medium-sized bowl, whisk the milk, eggs, orange juice and zest, and vanilla extract until smooth. Pour the mixture into a 9-by-13-inch baking dish.

2. Preheat a nonstick skillet to medium-high.

3. Working in batches, soak the bread in the custard mixture until it is saturated.

4. Melt the butter in the skillet, coating the entire cooking surface. Place the soaked bread in the skillet and cook until browned on both sides, about 4 minutes per side.

5. Sprinkle lightly with nutmeg. Serve immediately.

Serves 4 / **Per Serving**   Calories: 324   Protein: 14. 5 grams
Sugar: 9. 5 grams   Fat: 11. 5 grams

INGREDIENT TIP

Zest the orange using a fine grater. Grate only the top surface of the orange, avoiding the bitter white pith underneath.

Low-FODMAP Pancakes with Strawberry Topping

NUT-FREE   VEGETARIAN   SOY-FREE

Prep time: 10 minutes   **Cook time:** 15 minutes

Traditional pancakes aren't gluten-free, but your own homemade gluten-free baking mix allows you to make delicious low-FODMAP pancakes that taste just like those made with wheat flour. It's a good idea to keep some Gluten-Free Bisquick Pancake and Baking Mix in your pantry for those days when you don't have time to mix up your own.

1 cup Gluten-Free Baking Mix (page 201)

1 cup lactose-free whole milk

2 tablespoons canola oil

1 large egg

2 tablespoons unsalted butter

3 cups frozen sliced strawberries

$\frac{1}{2}$ cup sugar

1. Preheat the oven to 200°F.

2. Measure the baking mix into a medium-sized bowl.

3. In another bowl, whisk together the milk, canola oil, and egg until well combined.

4. Pour the wet ingredients into the baking mix, and stir with a spoon until just combined. You may notice some streaks of baking mix remaining in the batter.

5. Heat a nonstick skillet over medium-high heat. Melt the butter in the skillet.

6. Pour the pancake batter by the $\frac{1}{4}$ cup into the hot skillet.

7. Cook the pancakes on one side until bubbles show through the top of the batter, 3 to 4 minutes. Flip the pancakes and cook until done, another 3 to 4 minutes. Continue cooking the pancakes until all of the batter is gone.

8. Meanwhile, in a medium-sized saucepan over medium-high heat, bring the strawberries and sugar to a simmer, stirring frequently. Cook until the sugar dissolves, about 4 minutes.

9. Spoon the warm strawberry topping over the pancakes and serve.

....

Serves 4 / **Per Serving**   Calories: 333   Protein: 5 grams
Sugar: 33 grams   Fat: 14 grams

Low-FODMAP Breakfast Sausage

NUT-FREE PALEO-FRIENDLY DAIRY-FREE SOY-FREE

Prep time: 10 minutes   **Cook time:** 15 minutes

Some premade sausages contain ingredients that aren't low-FODMAP, such as high-fructose corn syrup (HFCS), garlic, and onions. You can easily make your own low-FODMAP breakfast sausage and then use it in other recipes. This sausage calls for ground pork, but you can also substitute ground turkey or chicken for a leaner sausage.

    2 teaspoons light brown sugar
    1 teaspoon dried sage
    $\frac{1}{2}$ teaspoon sea salt
    $\frac{1}{2}$ teaspoon freshly ground black pepper
    $\frac{1}{4}$ teaspoon dried marjoram
    $\frac{1}{4}$ teaspoon dried rosemary
    $\frac{1}{8}$ teaspoon red pepper flakes
    Pinch cayenne pepper
    1 pound ground pork

1. In a small bowl, whisk together the brown sugar, sage, salt, pepper, marjoram, rosemary, red pepper flakes, and cayenne until well combined.

2. Place the pork in a medium-sized bowl. Add the spice mixture.

3. Mix gently, using your hands, until well combined. Form the mixture into 8 patties.

4. Heat a large skillet over medium-high heat and cook the patties, turning once, until they are cooked through, about 15 minutes. Serve.

Serves 4 / **Per Serving**   Calories: 240   Fat: 18 grams
Sugar: 2. 5 grams   Protein: 20 grams

Breakfast Burritos with Eggs, Sausage, and Peppers

NUT-FREE   SOY-FREE

Prep time: 10 minutes   **Cook time:** 15 minutes

These Tex-Mex burritos make a hearty, delicious breakfast. Use the Low-FODMAP Breakfast Sausage recipe on page 72, but do not form the mixture into patties. Instead, cook the sausage as bulk sausage, breaking it up in the pan as you cook it. If desired, serve the burritos topped with Fresh Salsa (page 128).

8 (6-inch) corn tortillas

8 ounces Low-FODMAP Breakfast Sausage (page 72)

1 green bell pepper, seeded and chopped

3 scallions (green part only), chopped

6 large eggs, beaten

$\frac{1}{4}$ cup shredded cheddar cheese

1. Preheat the oven to 350°F.

2. Wrap the corn tortillas in foil, and place them in the oven directly on the rack. Bake the corn tortillas until they are heated through, about 15 minutes.

3. Meanwhile, place the sausage in a large nonstick skillet over medium-high heat and cook, breaking up the sausage with a wooden spoon, until it browns, about 5 minutes.

4. Add the pepper and scallion greens and cook, stirring occasionally, until the vegetables are soft, 3 to 4 minutes. ➤

Breakfast Burritos with Eggs, Sausage, and Peppers continued

5. Reduce the heat to medium and pour the beaten eggs into the pan. Cook, stirring constantly and scrambling the eggs, until set, about 4 minutes.

6. Spoon an equal portion of the egg-sausage mixture onto each warm tortilla. Top with the cheddar cheese and serve.

....

Serves 4 / **Per Serving**   Calories: 378   Protein: 14 grams
Sugar: 2 grams   Fat: 14 grams

WARNING

When using scallions, use only the green part, as the white part contains FODMAPs.

Ham, Egg, and Swiss Crustless Quiche

NUT-FREE SOY-FREE

Prep time: 10 minutes   **Cook time:** 30 minutes

This quiche doesn't have a crust like a traditional quiche. It uses chopped ham, although you can also substitute chopped bacon or cooked sausage if you wish. Leftovers keep up to 4 days when stored in a tightly sealed container in the refrigerator, and you can easily reheat them in the microwave the next day. Serve with melon slices.

6 large eggs, beaten

$1\frac{1}{2}$ cups lactose-free whole milk

1 teaspoon salt

$\frac{1}{4}$ teaspoon freshly ground black pepper

1 cup chopped ham

$1\frac{1}{2}$ cups shredded Swiss cheese

1. Preheat the oven to 350°F. Spray a 9-inch deep-dish pie plate with nonstick cooking spray and set aside.

2. In a large bowl, whisk together the eggs, milk, salt, and pepper. Fold in the ham and Swiss cheese until just combined.

3. Pour the mixture into the prepared pie plate. Bake until the eggs are set, about 30 minutes.

4. Allow the quiche to rest for 10 minutes before cutting into wedges and serving.

Serves 6 / Per Serving Calories: 215   Protein: 19 grams
Sugar: 1 gram   Fat: 14. 5 grams

Huevos Rancheros

NUT-FREE   VEGETARIAN   DAIRY-FREE   SOY-FREE

Prep time: 15 minutes   **Cook time:** 15 minutes

This Mexican breakfast gets your day off to a spicy start. While huevos rancheros recipes usually call for onions, in this recipe you will use the greens from scallions to get onion flavor without the FODMAPs. Be sure to remove the white part of the scallion entirely.

4 (6-inch) corn tortillas

2 tablespoons Garlic Oil (page 220)

4 scallions (green part only), chopped

2 medium tomatoes, chopped

1 (4-ounce) can chopped jalapeño peppers, drained

4 large eggs

Sea salt

Freshly ground black pepper

¼ cup chopped fresh cilantro, for garnish

1. Preheat the oven to 350°F.

2. Wrap the corn tortillas in foil and place them in the oven directly on the rack. Bake the corn tortillas until they are heated through, about 15 minutes.

3. Meanwhile, heat 1 tablespoon of the garlic oil in a sauté pan over medium-high heat. Add the scallion greens and cook until soft, about 4 minutes. Stir in the tomatoes and jalapeños and cook until warmed through.

4. Heat the remaining 1 tablespoon garlic oil in a nonstick skillet over medium heat, swirling to coat the pan.

5. Crack the eggs into the pan one at a time. Season the eggs with salt and pepper, and cook until the whites are set and the yolks remain slightly runny, about 4 minutes.

6. To assemble, place a corn tortilla on each plate. Top each with one-quarter of the tomato sauce and place a fried egg on top of the sauce. Garnish with the cilantro and serve.

Serves 4 / **Per Serving**   Calories: 208   Protein: 7 grams
Sugar: 3 grams   Fat: 13 grams

Eggs Benedict

Prep time: 15 minutes   **Cook time:** 15 minutes

*Eggs Benedict has been an American classic breakfast since the 1800s.
The traditional recipe calls for a poached egg and Canadian bacon on top of a
buttered, toasted English muffin, topped with rich hollandaise sauce. This version
replaces the English muffin with gluten-free sandwich bread. The recipe also calls
for a simplified version of hollandaise sauce you can make in the blender.*

FOR THE HOLLANDAISE SAUCE

3 large egg yolks

1 tablespoon freshly squeezed lemon juice

$\frac{1}{4}$ teaspoon Dijon mustard

Dash cayenne pepper

$\frac{1}{2}$ cup unsalted butter, melted and still hot

FOR THE EGGS

4 slices gluten-free sandwich bread

2 tablespoons unsalted butter

4 thick slices Canadian bacon

1 teaspoon white vinegar

4 large eggs

TO MAKE THE HOLLANDAISE SAUCE:

1. In the jar of a blender, combine the egg yolks, lemon juice, mustard, and cayenne. Blend until well combined, 5 to 10 seconds.

2. With the blender running on high, pour the hot butter in a thin stream through the hole in the lid until the butter is incorporated. The sauce will thicken and emulsify.

3. Using a rubber spatula, scrape the sauce into a medium-sized bowl. Place the bowl in a large bowl of hot water to keep the sauce warm while you finish preparing the other ingredients.

1. Toast the bread and spread each slice with $\frac{1}{2}$ tablespoon of the butter. Place the buttered toast on four serving plates.

2. In a large sauté pan, fry the Canadian bacon until it is crisp around the edges, about 3 minutes per side.

3. While the bacon cooks, place about 3 inches of water in a large saucepan and bring it to a simmer over medium heat. Add the vinegar. Break 1 egg into a custard cup and then slide the egg from the cup into the simmering water. Repeat with the remaining 3 eggs. Poach the eggs until the whites set, about 3 minutes. Remove the eggs carefully from the water with a slotted spoon.

4. To assemble the Eggs Benedict, top each piece of toast with a slice of Canadian bacon and a poached egg. Spoon the warm hollandaise sauce over the top and serve.

Serves 4 / **Per Serving**   Calories: 507   Protein: 22 grams
Sugar: 2 grams   Fat: 41 grams

WARNING

Read mustard labels carefully as many brands contain wheat flour.

Potato and Kale Frittata

NUT-FREE   VEGETARIAN   SOY-FREE

Prep time: 10 minutes   **Cook time:** 25 minutes

A frittata is the Italian version of an omelet. Use a sauté pan with an oven-safe handle, because at the end of cooking you will transfer the frittata to the broiler to brown on top and puff slightly. Cut the frittata into wedges and serve with fruit.

2 tablespoons Garlic Oil (page 220)

2 medium red potatoes, cut into $\frac{1}{2}$-inch dice

4 scallions (green part only), chopped

2 cups chopped kale

6 large eggs

$\frac{1}{4}$ cup lactose-free whole milk

$\frac{3}{4}$ teaspoon salt

$\frac{1}{4}$ teaspoon freshly ground black pepper

$\frac{1}{4}$ cup Parmesan cheese

1. Preheat the broiler.

2. In a 12-inch oven-safe sauté pan, heat the garlic oil over medium-high heat until it shimmers. Add the potatoes, scallion greens, and kale. Cook until they start to brown, about 6 minutes.

3. Reduce the heat to low. Continue cooking the potatoes and scallion greens until the potatoes are completely soft, about 10 more minutes. Return the temperature to medium-high.

4. While the vegetables cook, whisk the eggs, milk, salt, and pepper in a medium-sized bowl until well combined.

5. Pour the eggs over the vegetables in the pan and cook until the eggs are set around the edges, about 5 minutes. As the eggs set around the edges, use a spatula to gently pull the edges away from the side of the pan. Tilt the pan and allow the egg mixture to run into the spaces left around the edges. Do this until most of the runny egg mixture has been moved to the edges of the pan.

6. When the eggs have set around the edges again, sprinkle the frittata with the Parmesan cheese.

7. Place the pan under the broiler and allow it to cook until the cheese melts and the eggs puff, about 4 minutes. Cut into wedges and serve.

....

Serves 4 / **Per Serving**   Calories: 293   Protein: 18. 5 grams
Sugar: 3 grams   Fat: 17 grams

Poached Eggs on Red Potato Hash

NUT-FREE VEGETARIAN PALEO-FRIENDLY DAIRY-FREE SOY-FREE

Prep time: 10 minutes   **Cook time:** 15 minutes

A ¼-inch dice on the red potatoes allows this hash to cook quickly. If you have a mandoline slicer, this will allow you to cut the potatoes evenly and quickly, although you can also use a knife. Keep the skin on the potatoes, as it adds fiber and flavor.

2 tablespoons Garlic Oil (page 220)

4 medium red potatoes, cut into ¼-inch dice

½ teaspoon sea salt

¼ teaspoon freshly ground black pepper

1 teaspoon white vinegar

4 large eggs

¼ cup chopped fresh chives

1. In a large sauté pan, heat the garlic oil over medium-high heat until it is shimmering. Add the potatoes to the pan. Season them with the salt and pepper. Cook, stirring frequently, until the potatoes are soft and well browned, about 10 minutes.

2. While the potatoes cook, fill a large saucepan with about 3 inches of water and bring to a simmer over medium heat. Add the vinegar to the simmering water.

3. Crack 1 egg into a custard cup and carefully slip the egg into the simmering water. Repeat with each egg. Allow the eggs to simmer until the whites are set, about 4 minutes.

4. Divide the potatoes among four plates. Top with the poached eggs. Sprinkle with the chives and serve.

Serves 4 / Per Serving   Calories: 286   Protein: 9 grams
Sugar: 1. 5 grams   Fat: 9 grams

Fried Eggs on Sautéed Spinach and Red Peppers

NUT-FREE   VEGETARIAN   PALEO-FRIENDLY   DAIRY-FREE   SOY-FREE

Prep time: 5 minutes   **Cook time:** 10 minutes

If you prefer, you can use green, yellow, or orange peppers. You can also replace spinach with other low-FODMAP greens, such as Belgian endive or kale.

2 tablespoons Garlic Oil (page 220)

1 red bell pepper, seeded and cut into thin slices

2 cups baby spinach

2 large eggs

Sea salt

Freshly ground black pepper

2 teaspoons balsamic vinegar

1. In a large sauté pan, heat the garlic oil over medium-high heat until it shimmers. Add the bell pepper and cook, stirring frequently, until soft and starting to brown, about 5 minutes. Add the spinach and cook until it wilts, about 3 minutes.

2. Reduce the heat to medium. Arrange the vegetables into two piles in the pan, with a hole in the middle of each pile.

3. Carefully crack an egg into each hole.

4. Allow the eggs to cook until the whites are set, about 4 minutes.

5. Use a spatula to carefully transfer each nest with its egg to a plate.

6. Season with salt and pepper. Drizzle with the balsamic vinegar and serve.

Serves 2 / Per Serving   Calories: 215   Protein: 19 grams
Sugar: 2 grams   Fat: 19 grams

Lunch

Spinach, Strawberry, and Walnut Salad

VEGETARIAN   SOY-FREE

Prep time: 5 minutes   **Cook time:** None

Sliced red strawberries and bright green spinach make this a very pretty salad. If you take it to lunch, pack the salad separately from the vinaigrette and toss it with the vinaigrette just before eating. The Balsamic Dijon Dressing on page 222 is the perfect accompaniment for the salad.

1 (9-ounce) bag baby spinach

1 cup sliced strawberries

1 ounce Parmesan cheese, shaved

$\frac{1}{2}$ cup walnut pieces

Freshly ground black pepper

$\frac{1}{4}$ cup Balsamic Dijon Dressing (page 222)

In a large bowl, combine the baby spinach, strawberries, cheese, and walnuts. Grind pepper over the top. Add the vinaigrette and toss to combine. Serve.

Serves 2 / Per Serving   Calories: 409   Protein: 13 grams
Sugar: 4 grams   Fat: 27 g

INGREDIENT VARIATIONS

If you like, you can replace the Parmesan cheese with an equal amount of gorgonzola cheese, which has a sharper flavor.

Greek Salad with Mint and Cucumber

NUT-FREE VEGETARIAN SOY-FREE

Prep time: 10 minutes **Cook time:** None

Greek salad traditionally contains red onions. Since onions contain FODMAPs, this salad uses scallion greens to provide onion flavor. The vinaigrette is made with mint and lemon juice, adding vibrant Greek flavors to a fresh and colorful salad.

1 head lettuce, torn into bite-sized pieces
1 cucumber, chopped
1 cup quartered green olives
24 cherry tomatoes
1 yellow bell pepper, seeded and chopped
2 cups crumbled feta cheese
$\frac{1}{4}$ cup olive oil
Juice of 1 lemon
1 tablespoon chopped fresh mint
$\frac{1}{2}$ teaspoon dried oregano
Pinch sea salt
Pinch freshly ground black pepper

1. In a large bowl, combine the lettuce, cucumber, olives, tomatoes, bell pepper, and feta cheese.

2. In a small bowl, whisk the olive oil, lemon juice, mint, oregano, sea salt, and pepper until combined.

3. Pour the vinaigrette over the salad and toss to combine. Serve.

Serves 4 / **Per Serving** Calories: 507 Protein: 19 grams
Sugar: 25 grams Fat: 33 grams

Arugula Salad with Feta, Olives, and Heirloom Tomatoes

NUT-FREE   VEGETARIAN   SOY-FREE

Prep time: 5 minutes   **Cook time:** None

Arugula has a nice, peppery flavor that works well with the other ingredients in this salad. If you like, you can replace the black olives with any other type of olive of your choice. If heirloom tomatoes aren't in season, you can opt for a hothouse or beefsteak tomato.

9 ounces arugula

1 heirloom tomato, seeded and chopped

$\frac{1}{2}$ cup crumbled feta cheese

$\frac{1}{2}$ cup sliced black olives

$\frac{1}{4}$ cup Garlic-Basil Vinaigrette (page 221)

In a medium-sized bowl, toss the arugula, tomato, feta cheese, and olives until well combined. Pour the vinaigrette over the salad just before serving.

Serves 3 / **Per Serving**   Calories: 377   Protein: 4. 5 grams
Sugar: 2 grams   Fat: 34 grams

Chef Salad with Turkey, Ham, and Ranch Dressing

NUT-FREE   SOY-FREE

Prep time: 10 minutes   **Cook time:** None

To prepare this salad ahead of time, cut the meat and vegetables and prepare the dressing the night before. Store the meat, vegetables, and dressing in separate containers in the refrigerator until ready to serve.

- 1 head romaine lettuce, torn into pieces
- 3 ounces deli-sliced turkey, chopped
- 3 ounces deli-sliced ham, chopped
- 2 hard-boiled eggs, peeled and chopped
- 4 scallions (green part only), chopped
- 1 cucumber, peeled and chopped
- 1 tomato, seeded and chopped
- 6 tablespoons Ranch Dressing (page 226)

In a large bowl, combine the romaine lettuce, turkey, ham, eggs, scallion greens, cucumber, and tomato. Toss with the ranch dressing to coat. Serve.

Serves 3 / **Per Serving**   Calories: 304   Protein: 16 grams
Sugar: 6 grams   Fat: 24 grams

Salade Niçoise

NUT-FREE   PALEO-FRIENDLY   DAIRY-FREE   SOY-FREE

Prep time: 20 minutes   **Cook time:** 15 minutes

This traditional French salad from Nice is typically served on a bed of butter lettuce. While Salade Niçoise often has both tuna and anchovies, this salad calls for only tuna. (You can also substitute grilled fresh tuna for the canned tuna.) Present the salad with each vegetable in its own separate pile atop the butter lettuce with the vinaigrette drizzled over the top.

FOR THE VINAIGRETTE
$3/4$ cup extra-virgin olive oil

$1/2$ cup freshly squeezed lemon juice

2 tablespoons chopped fresh chives

2 tablespoons minced fresh basil

1 tablespoon minced fresh thyme

1 teaspoon Dijon mustard

Salt

Freshly ground black pepper

FOR THE SALAD
8 baby red potatoes, quartered

8 ounces green beans, halved

2 heads butter lettuce

8 ounces water-packed tuna, drained

6 hard-boiled eggs, peeled and cut into quarters pole-to-pole

1 cup cherry tomatoes

$1/4$ cup halved Niçoise olives

Sea salt

Freshly ground black pepper

TO MAKE THE VINAIGRETTE

1. In a small bowl, combine the oil, lemon juice, chives, basil, thyme, and mustard. Add salt and pepper and whisk until emulsified. Set aside.

TO MAKE THE SALAD

1. Place the potatoes in a large pot of water and bring to a boil over high heat. Boil until the potatoes are soft, about 6 minutes. Remove the potatoes from the water with a slotted spoon and transfer them to a large bowl. Toss them with ¼ cup of the vinaigrette. Set aside.

2. Return the water to the boil and add the green beans. Cook until the green beans start to soften but remain crisp, about 4 minutes. Remove the beans from the water with a slotted spoon and plunge them into ice water to stop cooking. Drain and set aside.

3. Arrange the lettuce leaves on a large platter. On the lettuce, arrange the potatoes, green beans, tuna, eggs, cherry tomatoes, and olives in separate mounds. Season with salt and pepper. Drizzle with the remaining vinaigrette and serve.

Serves 4 / **Per Serving** Calories: 642 Protein: 24 grams
Sugar: 9 grams Fat: 49 grams

Cobb Salad

NUT-FREE   SOY-FREE

Prep time: 20 minutes   **Cook time:** 8 minutes

The Cobb Salad is an American classic named for Hollywood Brown Derby Restaurant owner Robert Howard Cobb. Traditional Cobb salads have avocados, but this version leaves them off because avocados contain FODMAPs. Even without the avocados, however, there are still plenty of delicious ingredients to keep this salad interesting.

FOR THE VINAIGRETTE

$\frac{1}{3}$ cup red wine vinegar

1 tablespoon Dijon mustard

1 teaspoon sugar

1 tablespoon finely chopped fresh chives

$\frac{1}{2}$ teaspoon salt

$\frac{1}{4}$ teaspoon freshly ground black pepper

$\frac{2}{3}$ cups olive oil

$\frac{1}{2}$ cup finely crumbled blue cheese

FOR THE SALAD

6 bacon slices

2 heads romaine lettuce, torn into bite-sized pieces

1 boneless, skinless chicken breast, grilled, cooled, and cubed

2 hard-boiled eggs, peeled and finely chopped

1 beefsteak or heirloom tomato, seeded and finely chopped

TO MAKE THE VINAIGRETTE

1. In a small bowl, whisk the red wine vinegar, Dijon mustard, sugar, chives, salt, and pepper until well combined. Slowly pour in the olive oil in a thin stream, whisking as you pour. Stir in the blue cheese. Set aside.

1. In a large sauté pan over medium-high heat, cook the bacon until it is browned and crisp, about 4 minutes per side. Drain on paper towels.

2. Arrange the lettuce on a large platter. Crumble the bacon and arrange in a small pile on top of the lettuce. Arrange the chicken, eggs, and tomato in groupings on top of the lettuce.

3. Whisk the vinaigrette a final time to recombine and drizzle it over the salad. Serve.

Serves 4 / **Per Serving**   Calories: 503   Protein: 23 grams
Sugar: 5 grams   Fat: 43 grams

TIME-SAVING TIP

Cook the chicken ahead of time and store it in the refrigerator for up to 4 days. Or, even easier, you can purchase a rotisserie chicken or deli-sliced chicken for this salad.

Ham and Peppers Chopped Salad

NUT-FREE   SOY-FREE

Prep time: 20 minutes   **Cook time:** None

This traditional Italian chopped salad calls for sweet red peppers, which add a nice crunch. The Italian-style dressing serves as a counterpoint for the peppers and meat. If you'd prefer a lower-fat salad, you can replace the ham with chicken or turkey. Use ¼-inch dice for all of the ingredients in this salad.

FOR THE VINAIGRETTE

¼ cup olive oil

2 tablespoons red wine vinegar

2 tablespoons grated Parmesan cheese

¼ teaspoon salt

⅛ teaspoon freshly ground black pepper

FOR THE SALAD

3 cups romaine lettuce, chopped

2 medium beefsteak or heirloom tomatoes, seeded and diced

2 red bell peppers, seeded and diced

3 scallions (green part only), diced

½ cup diced black olives

¼ cup diced pepperoncini

12 ounces baked ham, diced

TO MAKE THE VINAIGRETTE

1. In a small bowl, whisk together the olive oil, red wine vinegar, Parmesan cheese, salt, and pepper. Set aside.

1. In a large bowl, combine the romaine lettuce, tomatoes, red peppers, scallion greens, black olives, pepperoncini, and ham. Toss to combine.

2. Whisk the vinaigrette one final time to recombine and pour it over the salad, tossing to combine. Serve.

....

Serves 4 / **Per Serving**   Calories: 363   Protein: 16. 5 grams
Sugar: 4 grams   Fat: 29. 4 grams

Chicken Salad with Grapes

PALEO-FRIENDLY   DAIRY-FREE   SOY-FREE

Prep time: 10 minutes   **Cook time:** None

This salad is a play on the classic Waldorf salad. Waldorf salads contain apples, which contain FODMAPs, so this salad replaces the apples with grapes. It is topped with a creamy dressing. Although the recipe specifies green grapes, you can choose any type of seedless grapes you wish.

12 ounces boneless, skinless chicken breast, grilled and cut into $\frac{1}{2}$-inch cubes

2 celery stalks, chopped

$\frac{1}{2}$ cup chopped fennel

1 cup halved green grapes

$\frac{1}{2}$ cup chopped walnuts

1 cup Low-FODMAP Mayonnaise (page 224)

$\frac{1}{2}$ teaspoon salt

$\frac{1}{2}$ teaspoon freshly ground black pepper

4 large butter lettuce leaves

In a large bowl, toss together the chicken, celery, fennel, green grapes, and walnuts until well combined. Add the mayonnaise, salt, and pepper. Toss again to combine. Serve the salad in the butter lettuce leaves.

Serves 4 / **Per Serving**   Calories: 507   Protein: 29 grams
Sugar: 8 grams   Fat: 35 grams

WARNING

If you choose to use store-bought mayonnaise instead of making your own, read the label carefully to ensure it does not contain high-fructose corn syrup (HFCS).

Pasta Salad with Ham and Vegetables

NUT-FREE   SOY-FREE

Prep time: 10 minutes   **Cook time:** 10 minutes

Just because you can't eat wheat doesn't mean you can't enjoy pasta—simply use gluten-free rotini in this salad. The recipe calls for optional artichoke hearts. Artichoke hearts are allowed in small amounts on a low-FODMAP diet, but don't add any more than noted in the recipe.

8 ounces gluten-free rotini

12 ounces ham, cubed

1 cup halved cherry tomatoes

1 green bell pepper, seeded and chopped

4 scallions (green part only), chopped

$\frac{1}{2}$ cup chopped black olives

$\frac{1}{4}$ cup chopped artichoke hearts (optional)

$\frac{1}{4}$ cup fresh basil leaves, torn into pieces

4 ounces mozzarella cheese, cubed

$\frac{1}{2}$ cup Garlic-Basil Vinaigrette (page 221)

1. Bring a large pot of water to a rolling boil over high heat. Add the pasta, stir, and return the water to the boil. Cook the pasta according to the package directions until al dente, 7 to 9 minutes.

2. Drain the pasta and rinse it with cool water. Allow it to cool completely before continuing.   ➤

Pasta Salad with Ham and Vegetables continued

3. In a large bowl, combine the cooled pasta, ham, cherry tomatoes, bell pepper, scallion greens, black olives, artichoke hearts (if using), basil leaves, and mozzarella. Toss well.

4. Add the vinaigrette and toss to combine. Serve.

Serves 4 / **Per Serving**   Calories: 608   Protein: 29 grams
Sugar: 3 grams   Fat: 37 grams

INGREDIENT TIP

If you can find it, use fresh mozzarella that is packed in water. It has much better flavor than packaged mozzarella. You may be able to find it at the salad bar or in the specialty cheese section of your grocery store.

Vegetable Stock

NUT-FREE   VEGETARIAN   VEGAN   PALEO-FRIENDLY   DAIRY-FREE   SOY-FREE

Prep time: 10 minutes   **Cook time:** 40 minutes

This vegetable stock can be sipped as a meal or snack, or you can use it as the basis for other soups and recipes found in this book. Homemade vegetable stock is an important part of low-FODMAP cooking, because premade stocks and broths commonly contain onions and garlic. Although the cooking time is long to extract the most flavor from the vegetables, it requires little attention, and prep is easy. Prepare it on the weekends, and then store it in your refrigerator or freezer in 2-cup portions for use when you need it.

2 tablespoons Garlic Oil (page 220)

4 celery stalks, cut into 1-inch chunks

4 large carrots, peeled and cut into 1-inch chunks

6 scallions (green part only), chopped

12 fresh parsley sprigs

12 fresh thyme sprigs

4 bay leaves

$1\frac{1}{2}$ teaspoons salt

12 cups water

1. In a large stockpot, heat the garlic oil over medium-high heat until it shimmers. Add the celery, carrots, and scallion greens. Cook, stirring occasionally, until the vegetables begin to brown, about 7 minutes.

2. Add the parsley, thyme, bay leaves, salt, and water and bring to a boil. Lower the heat and simmer, uncovered, for 30 minutes. ➤

Vegetable Stock continued

3. Strain the stock through a fine-mesh sieve into another pot. Cover and store in the refrigerator for up to 1 week or in the freezer for up to 3 months.

....

Makes 10 cups / **Per Serving (1 cup)** Calories: 25 Protein: 0 grams
Sugar: 2 grams Fat: 1 gram

SERVING SUGGESTION

When you're ready to use the stock, you can make a quick soup by simmering diced vegetables in the stock until they soften, about 5 minutes.

TIME-SAVING TIP

Make double batches of this stock so you only have to make it every few weeks. Freeze the stock in 2- or 4-cup containers for use in recipes.

Asian Ginger Chicken and Rice Soup

NUT-FREE   DAIRY-FREE   SOY-FREE

Prep time: 10 minutes   **Cook time:** 40 minutes

Ginger, star anise, and Chinese five-spice powder give this soup enticing Asian flavors. Use homemade Vegetable Stock (page 99), because store-bought stock usually contains onions. Prepare this soup on the weekend so it will be ready for busy weekday lunches.

2 tablespoons Garlic Oil (page 220)

12 ounces boneless, skinless chicken breast, cut into $\frac{1}{2}$-inch cubes

1 (1-inch) knob ginger, peeled and grated

3 scallions (green part only), minced

2 carrots, peeled and chopped

2 celery stalks, peeled and chopped

6 cups Vegetable Stock (page 99)

3 star anise

$\frac{1}{2}$ teaspoon Chinese five-spice powder

1 cup chopped bok choy

2 cups cooked white rice

1. In a large stockpot, warm the garlic oil over medium high heat until it shimmers. Add the chicken breast and cook until the meat is completely cooked through, about 8 minutes. Remove the chicken from the oil with a slotted spoon and transfer to a platter.

2. Add the ginger, scallion greens, carrots, and celery. Cook until the vegetables soften and begin to brown, about 6 minutes.   ➤

Asian Ginger Chicken and Rice Soup continued

3. Stir in the stock, scraping up any browned bits from the bottom of the pot.

4. Add the star anise and Chinese five-spice powder. Reduce the heat and simmer, uncovered, for 20 minutes.

5. Add the bok choy and rice. Return the chicken to the pot. Cook until the bok choy wilts, about 5 more minutes. Serve.

....

Serves 4 / **Per Serving**   Calories: 617   Protein: 42 grams
Sugar: 4 grams   Fat: 13 grams

Vegetable Soup with Ground Pork and Macaroni

NUT-FREE   DAIRY-FREE   SOY-FREE

Prep time: 15 minutes   **Cook time:** 25 minutes

This hearty soup is filled with vegetables and Italian seasonings. It also calls for gluten-free elbow macaroni. If you don't care for the vegetables in this soup, you can add any low-FODMAP vegetables you wish. Serve it topped with grated Parmesan cheese.

2 tablespoons Garlic Oil (page 220)

12 ounces ground pork

3 scallions (green part only), chopped

1 carrot, peeled and chopped

1 celery stalk, chopped

$\frac{1}{4}$ cup chopped fennel bulb

8 cups Vegetable Stock (page 99)

1 (8-ounce) can fire-roasted tomatoes, drained and chopped

1 zucchini, chopped

4 ounces green beans, chopped

4 ounces gluten-free elbow macaroni

2 tablespoons dried Italian herb blend

Sea salt

Freshly ground black pepper

1. In a large stockpot, heat the garlic oil over medium-high heat until it shimmers. Add the pork and cook, breaking up the pork with a spoon, until it browns, about 7 minutes.

2. Remove the pork from the fat with a slotted spoon, and set it aside to drain on paper towels.   ➤

Vegetable Soup with Ground Pork and Macaroni continued

3. In the oil that remains in the pot, cook the scallion greens, carrot, celery, and fennel until they soften and begin to brown, about 7 minutes.

4. Add the vegetable stock and tomatoes, scraping up any browned bits from the bottom of the pan.

5. Add the cooked pork, zucchini, green beans, elbow macaroni, and Italian seasoning. Bring the soup to a boil and cook, stirring occasionally, until the elbow macaroni is al dente and the vegetables soften, about 9 minutes.

6. Season with salt and pepper and serve.

....

Serves 4 / **Per Serving** Calories: 550 Protein: 29 grams
Sugar: 4 grams Fat: 34 grams

TIME-SAVING TIP

Purchase precut vegetables from the salad bar at your local grocery store to save valuable prep time. Store them tightly sealed in the refrigerator until you're ready to use them. They should keep for up to 4 days.

Ground Beef and Cabbage Soup

NUT-FREE   PALEO-FRIENDLY   DAIRY-FREE   SOY-FREE

Prep time: 10 minutes   **Cook time:** 25 minutes

This soup makes a great lunch. Ground beef gives it plenty of protein, and cabbage adds fiber that makes the soup satisfying. Choose leaner ground beef to lower the fat content of the soup. Serve with gluten-free crackers or a slice of toast made from gluten-free bread.

2 tablespoons Garlic Oil (page 220)

12 ounces lean ground beef

6 scallions (green part only), chopped

1 carrot, peeled and diced

1 celery stalk, diced

1 red bell pepper, seeded and diced

2 tomatoes, chopped

8 cups Vegetable Stock (page 99)

3 cups shredded green cabbage

1 tablespoon dried thyme

Sea salt

Freshly ground black pepper

1. In a large stockpot, heat the garlic oil over medium-high heat until it shimmers. Add the ground beef and cook, breaking up the beef with a spoon, until it is browned, about 6 minutes. Remove the ground beef with a slotted spoon and set aside to drain on paper towels.

2. In the oil that remains, add the scallion greens, carrot, celery, and bell pepper. Cook, stirring frequently, until the vegetables soften, about 6 minutes. Add the tomatoes and cook for 2 more minutes.   ➤

Ground Beef and Cabbage Soup continued

3. Add the vegetable stock, scraping up any browned bits from the bottom of the pot. Add the cabbage, thyme, and cooked ground beef. Simmer until the cabbage softens, about 10 minutes.

4. Season with salt and pepper and serve.

....

Serves 4 / **Per Serving**   Calories: 342   Protein: 37 grams
Sugar: 7 grams   Fat: 15 grams

TIME-SAVING TIP

You can save the time spent shredding cabbage by purchasing bagged coleslaw mix or preshredded cabbage. You can find it in the produce section of the grocery store.

Lettuce Wrap with Shrimp Salad

NUT-FREE   PALEO-FRIENDLY   DAIRY-FREE   SOY-FREE

Prep time: 10 minutes   **Cook time:** None

Instead of using bread or a tortilla for a sandwich, this recipe uses a large piece of lettuce to wrap around delicious shrimp salad. While you can use store-bought mayonnaise that doesn't contain high-fructose corn syrup (HFCS), the homemade mayonnaise called for here is creamy and delicious.

1 pound cooked shrimp

1 celery stalk, finely diced

3 scallions (green part only), finely chopped

$\frac{1}{2}$ cup Low-FODMAP Mayonnaise (page 224)

2 tablespoons chopped fresh tarragon

2 teaspoons freshly squeezed lemon juice

$\frac{1}{4}$ teaspoon Worcestershire sauce

4 large lettuce leaves

1. In a large bowl, combine the shrimp, celery, and scallions.

2. In a small bowl, whisk together the mayonnaise, tarragon, lemon juice, and Worcestershire sauce. Pour the mayonnaise mixture over the shrimp mixture and stir to combine.

3. Spoon the shrimp salad into the lettuce leaves. Wrap the leaves around the shrimp salad to eat.

Serves 4 / **Per Serving**   Calories: 259   Protein: 27 grams
Sugar: 3 grams   Fat: 12 grams

Open-Face Bacon, Tomato, and Cheddar Sandwich

NUT-FREE SOY-FREE

Prep time: 5 minutes   **Cook time:** 10 minutes

Salty bacon and sweet tomatoes are a delicious combination. Enjoy this sandwich when heirloom tomatoes are in season for the best results. If you can't find farmers' market heirloom tomatoes, you can substitute hothouse tomatoes that are available year-round at the grocery store. Serve with a side of Baked Garlic Oil Potato Chips (page 122).

4 slices gluten-free sandwich bread

2 tablespoons Garlic Oil (page 220)

6 bacon slices, halved crosswise

2 heirloom tomatoes, cut into thick slices

4 ounces cheddar cheese, grated

1. Preheat your broiler.

2. Toast the bread. Brush one side of each slice of toast with the garlic oil. Place on a baking sheet.

3. In a large nonstick skillet, cook the bacon until it is browned and crisp, about 6 minutes. Drain it on paper towels.

4. Place 1 or 2 tomato slices on each slice of toast. Place three half slices of bacon on top of the tomato. Top with the grated cheddar.

5. Broil until the cheese melts, 2 to 3 minutes. Serve.

Serves 4 / Per Serving   Calories: 308   Protein: 14 grams
Sugar: 2 grams   Fat: 18 grams

Chicken and Spicy Sprout Wrap

NUT-FREE   SOY-FREE

Prep time: 10 minutes   **Cook time:** None

Wraps are quick and easy. This recipe calls for cream cheese, which is a moderate-FODMAP food. Be sure you don't use any more than 2 tablespoons per wrap, which is the maximum allowable for a low-FODMAP diet. Higher amounts have too much lactose and may cause problems. If you have trouble finding spicy sprouts, substitute them with other types of sprouts or a leafy green like arugula.

6 tablespoons cream cheese

1 tablespoon Low-FODMAP Mayonnaise (page 224)

½ teaspoon Dijon mustard

2 tablespoons chopped fresh chives

3 scallions (green part only), minced

½ yellow bell pepper, seeded and minced

8 (6-inch) corn tortillas

12 ounces deli-sliced chicken

1 cup spicy sprouts

1 tomato, seeded and chopped

1. In a small bowl, mix the cream cheese, mayonnaise, and Dijon mustard until well combined. Stir in the chives, scallions, and bell peppers.

2. Spread the cream cheese mixture on the corn tortillas. Divide the chicken among the corn tortillas. Top with the sprouts and tomatoes.

3. Roll the tortillas around the filling and serve.

Serves 4 / **Per Serving**   Calories: 182   Protein: 4. 5 grams
Sugar: 1 gram   Fat: 8 grams

Tuna Melt

NUT-FREE   SOY-FREE

Prep time: 10 minutes   **Cook time:** 5 minutes

Tuna melts are an American classic. Use water-packed tuna, which is lower in fat than its oil-packed counterpart. You can also make the following tuna salad completely Paleo-friendly by eliminating the cheese and gluten-free bread and instead serving it in a lettuce cup or wrap.

12 ounces water-packed tuna, drained
6 scallions (green part only), minced
2 medium celery stalks, minced
1 tablespoon minced Italian parsley
$\frac{1}{3}$ cup Low-FODMAP Mayonnaise (page 224)
Juice of 1 lemon
Freshly ground black pepper
4 slices gluten-free sandwich bread
4 ounces grated cheddar cheese

1. Preheat your broiler.

2. In a large bowl, mix the tuna, scallion greens, celery, and parsley.

3. In a small bowl, whisk together the mayonnaise, lemon juice, and black pepper. Pour the dressing over the tuna mixture and stir to combine.

4. Toast the bread and place it on a baking sheet. Top with the tuna salad and then the cheddar cheese.

5. Broil the sandwiches until the cheese melts and bubbles, 3 to 4 minutes. Serve.

Serves 4 / **Per Serving**   Calories: 418   Protein: 31 grams
Sugar: 2 grams   Fat: 21 grams

Spicy Egg Salad Sandwich

NUT-FREE   VEGETARIAN   DAIRY-FREE   SOY-FREE

Prep time: 10 minutes   **Cook time:** None

This egg salad has a twist, with spicy ingredients that ramp up the heat level. If you prefer to make this Paleo-friendly, you can serve the egg salad on a bed of lettuce.

8 slices gluten-free sandwich bread

$\frac{1}{2}$ cup Low-FODMAP Mayonnaise (page 224)

1 tablespoon Dijon mustard

2 teaspoons prepared horseradish

$\frac{1}{4}$ teaspoon hot pepper sauce

$\frac{1}{4}$ teaspoon cayenne pepper

6 hard-boiled eggs, peeled and chopped

1. Toast the bread.

2. In a medium-sized bowl, whisk together the mayonnaise, Dijon mustard, horseradish, hot pepper sauce, and cayenne. Carefully stir in the chopped eggs until well combined.

3. Divide the egg salad among four slices of toast. Top the sandwiches with the remaining toast and serve.

Serves 4 / **Per Serving**   Calories: 453   Protein: 13 grams
Sugar: 3 grams   Fat: 25 grams

INGREDIENT TIP

When selecting a hot pepper sauce, choose one that does not contain onion or garlic. One popular low-FODMAP option is Texas Pete's hot sauce.

Monte Cristo Sandwich

NUT-FREE   SOY-FREE

Prep time: 5 minutes   **Cook time:** 10 minutes

The Monte Cristo Sandwich is a variation of the traditional French croque monsieur. It is a delicious ham and cheese sandwich that is dipped in custard and then fried. It is similar to a savory French toast stuffed with ham and cheese. While this recipe calls for Swiss cheese, you can replace it with cheddar if you wish.

2 large eggs

$\frac{2}{3}$ cup lactose-free whole milk

Pinch sea salt

$\frac{1}{8}$ teaspoon freshly ground black pepper

8 slices gluten-free sandwich bread

1 tablespoon Dijon mustard

12 ounces deli-sliced ham

4 ounces Swiss cheese, grated

$\frac{1}{4}$ cup unsalted butter

1. In a medium bowl, whisk together the eggs, milk, salt, and pepper until smooth. Pour the mixture into a shallow dish.

2. Spread the bread slices with Dijon mustard. Top them with the ham and cheese, evenly divided among four pieces of bread. Top with the remaining four pieces of bread, and press them gently with your hand to flatten.

3. Dip the sandwiches in the custard mixture, turning to coat both pieces of bread.

4. Heat the butter in a large nonstick skillet over medium-high heat until it bubbles. Place the sandwiches in the butter and cook, without disturbing, for 4 minutes. Flip the sandwiches and cook the other side until the cheese melts and the custard sets, about 4 minutes more. Serve.

Serves 4 / **Per Serving**   Calories: 627   Protein: 29 grams
Sugar: 6 grams   Fat: 37 grams

Stuffed Baked Potato with Broccoli and Cheddar

NUT-FREE   VEGETARIAN   SOY-FREE

Prep time: 5 minutes   **Cook time:** 1 hour

The potatoes take a while to bake, but it is all passive time, and they can quickly be rewarmed in the microwave for weekday lunches. If you'd like more protein, you can add some rotisserie chicken to each potato.

4 medium russet potatoes

2 tablespoons Garlic Oil (page 220)

Sea salt

Freshly ground black pepper

2 cups broccoli florets

8 tablespoons unsalted butter

4 ounces cheddar cheese, shredded

1. Preheat the oven to 350°F.

2. Wash the potatoes and dry them thoroughly. Prick each potato several times with a fork. Rub the garlic oil all over the potatoes, and place them in a baking pan. Sprinkle with salt and pepper. Bake the potatoes until soft, about 1 hour.

3. Set a steamer basket in a medium-sized pot with just enough water to come up to the bottom of the steamer basket. Bring the water to a boil over high heat. Place the broccoli in the steamer basket, cover, and cook until the broccoli is tender, 5 to 6 minutes. ➤

Stuffed Baked Potato with Broccoli and Cheddar continued

4. When the potatoes are done, turn the broiler on. Split the potatoes down the side and pinch to open. Fluff the potato in the shell with a fork. Top each potato with 2 tablespoons of the butter and $\frac{1}{2}$ cup of the broccoli. Season with salt and pepper. Top with the cheddar cheese.

5. Place the potatoes under the broiler until the cheese melts, about 3 minutes.

....

Serves 4 / **Per Serving** Calories: 540 Protein: 12 grams
Sugar: 3 grams Fat: 40 grams

TIME-SAVING TIP

Bake the potatoes on the weekend and store, wrapped in foil, in the refrigerator for up to 4 days. Reheat in the microwave and proceed with the recipe.

6

Snacks

Baked Corn Tortilla Chips

NUT-FREE VEGETARIAN VEGAN DAIRY-FREE SOY-FREE

Prep time: 5 minutes   **Cook time:** 25 minutes

These corn tortilla chips can be used for snacking by themselves or with the dips found in this chapter. Use 6-inch corn tortillas. If you like, you can brush them with Garlic Oil (page 220) instead of plain oil and sprinkle them with sea salt for additional flavor. Store them for up to 1 week in a tightly sealed container.

12 (6-inch) corn tortillas
2 tablespoons olive oil
Sea salt (optional)

1. Preheat the oven to 350°F.

2. Slice the tortillas into six triangles each, and place them in a large bowl. Add the olive oil and sea salt (if using) and toss to coat.

3. Place the coated tortilla chips in a single layer on two baking sheets. Bake until the chips are browned and crisp, 20 to 25 minutes.

Serves 4 / **Per Serving**   Calories: 217   Protein: 4 grams
Sugar: 1 gram   Fat: 4 grams

WARNING

Limit these to about 18 chips per day; any more may cause IBS upset.

Baba Ghanoush

NUT-FREE   VEGETARIAN   VEGAN   PALEO-FRIENDLY   DAIRY-FREE   SOY-FREE

Prep time: 15 minutes   **Cook time:** 10 minutes

This eggplant dip is a traditional Middle Eastern snack. Traditional baba ghanoush calls for lots of garlic, which is replaced here with garlic oil. The recipe also leaves out the tahini, which is high in FODMAPs. Limit intake to less than 1 cup per day. Serve it with the Baked Corn Tortilla Chips on page 118, or stuff it into gluten-free pita bread. You can also use it as a dip for vegetables. Leftovers can be stored in a tightly sealed container in the refrigerator for up to 3 days.

1 large eggplant, peeled and cut into $\frac{1}{4}$-inch-thick slices

2 tablespoons olive oil

$\frac{1}{4}$ cup freshly squeezed lemon juice

$\frac{1}{4}$ teaspoon ground cumin

$\frac{1}{4}$ teaspoon sea salt

$\frac{1}{4}$ cup Garlic Oil (page 220)

1 tablespoon chopped fresh flat-leaf parsley

1. Heat the grill to high. Lightly brush the grate with oil.

2. Brush each slice of eggplant with olive oil and place it on the hot grill. Grill, flipping occasionally, until the slices are very soft and have grill marks, about 5 minutes per side.

3. Allow the eggplant to cool slightly, about 5 minutes.   ➤

4. Place the eggplant in a medium bowl and mash it with a fork. Add the lemon juice, cumin, and salt. Mix well. Taste and add additional salt, if necessary. Drizzle the eggplant with the garlic oil and sprinkle with the chopped parsley. Serve.

....

Serves 4 / **Per Serving**   Calories: 213   Protein: 1 gram
Sugar: 3 grams   Fat: 21 grams

INGREDIENT VARIATION

If you don't have a grill, you can roast the eggplant in a 450°F oven. To do this, keep the eggplant whole and unpeeled, and prick it all over with a fork. Roast on a baking sheet until the eggplant is soft, about 20 minutes. Allow the eggplant to cool and then remove the skin. Proceed with the recipe as indicated.

Spiced Popcorn

NUT-FREE   VEGETARIAN   SOY-FREE

Prep time: 5 minutes   **Cook time:** 5 minutes

Popcorn makes a great snack, but this popcorn is special because it's tossed with sweet and savory spices. While this recipe shows you how to pop the corn in a pot on the stove, you can also air-pop the corn and toss it with butter and spices. Avoid microwavable popcorn since it may contain additives that aggravate IBS.

2 tablespoons canola oil

$\frac{1}{2}$ cup popcorn kernels

$\frac{1}{4}$ cup unsalted butter, melted

$\frac{1}{2}$ teaspoon cayenne pepper

$\frac{1}{2}$ teaspoon ground cumin

$\frac{1}{2}$ teaspoon ground cinnamon

2 tablespoons brown sugar

1. Heat the canola oil in a heavy pot over high heat until it shimmers.

2. Add 1 kernel of popcorn and wait for it to pop. When the kernel pops, add the remaining popcorn and cover the pot.

3. Carefully shift the pot back and forth while maintaining contact with the stove top to stir the kernels. Cook until the popping slows to about 1 pop per second. Pour the popcorn into a large bowl.

4. In a small bowl, mix the melted butter, cayenne, cumin, cinnamon, and brown sugar. Pour the mixture over the popcorn. Serve immediately.

Serves 4 / Per Serving   Calories: 183   Protein: 0 grams
Sugar: 4. 4 grams   Fat: 18. 6 grams

Baked Garlic Oil Potato Chips

Prep time: 5 minutes   **Cook time:** 30 minutes

These potato chips are very versatile. This version has a garlic flavor, but you can also add other chopped herbs and spices such as rosemary or chives. If you prefer plain potato chips, just use plain olive oil instead of the garlic oil.

4 large russet potatoes, cut into ¼-inch-thick slices
3 tablespoons Garlic Oil (page 220)
Sea salt

1. Preheat the oven to 400°F. Line two baking sheets with parchment paper.

2. Place the potato slices in a large bowl. Toss them with the garlic oil and salt. Arrange the chips in a single layer on the baking sheets. Bake until the chips are golden, about 30 minutes. Serve.

Serves 4 / **Per Serving**   Calories: 345   Protein: 6 grams
Sugar: 4. 2 grams   Fat: 11 grams

Vanilla Chia Pudding with Blueberries

NUT-FREE   VEGETARIAN   VEGAN   DAIRY-FREE   SOY-FREE

Prep time: 5 minutes, plus overnight refrigeration   **Cook time:** None

Chia pudding makes a good snack because it is quick and very easy to make. It is also filling. When chia seeds soak in liquid, they swell and turn into a gel with a texture similar to tapioca. Top this pudding with fresh blueberries or any other low-FODMAP fruit.

2 cups unsweetened rice milk

$1/4$ cup sugar

$1/2$ teaspoon pure vanilla extract

$2/3$ cups chia seeds

1 cup fresh blueberries

1. In a medium-sized bowl, whisk together the rice milk, sugar, and vanilla until well combined.

2. Stir in the chia seeds. Allow the mixture to sit on the counter for 30 minutes. Then cover and refrigerate it overnight.

3. Before serving, stir in the blueberries.

Serves 4 / Per Serving   Calories: 169   Protein: 5 grams
Sugar: 16 grams   Fat: 8 grams

INGREDIENT TIP

This will keep in the refrigerator, tightly covered, for 3 days. Don't add the blueberries until just before serving.

Deviled Eggs

NUT-FREE   VEGETARIAN   PALEO-FRIENDLY   DAIRY-FREE   SOY-FREE

Prep time: 15 minutes   **Cook time:** 14 minutes

Deviled eggs are a North American favorite. They are also packed with protein. You can store them in a tightly sealed container in the refrigerator for up to 3 days. While this recipe has you spoon the filling into the egg whites, you can make prettier deviled eggs by placing the filling in a pastry bag and piping it into the eggs.

6 large eggs
$\frac{1}{4}$ cup Low-FODMAP Mayonnaise (page 224)
1 teaspoon white wine vinegar
1 teaspoon Dijon mustard
$\frac{1}{8}$ teaspoon salt
$\frac{1}{8}$ teaspoon freshly ground black pepper
Paprika

1. Place the eggs in a large pot in a single layer. Cover the eggs with water by at least 1 inch. Turn the burner on high and cook until the water comes to a boil.

2. Cover the pot and turn off the burner. Allow the eggs to sit, covered, for 14 minutes. Remove the eggs from the hot water and plunge them into a bowl of cold water to stop the cooking.

3. Carefully peel the eggs under running water.

4. Halve the eggs pole-to-pole. Carefully scoop out the egg yolks and place them in a medium-sized bowl. Place the whites on a plate with the cut sides up.

5. Mash the egg yolks with a fork. Stir in the mayonnaise, vinegar, mustard, salt, and pepper. Spoon the yolk mixture back into the cavities in the cooked egg whites. Sprinkle with paprika and serve.

Serves 4 / **Per Serving**   Calories: 153   Protein: 8. 5 grams
Sugar: 1. 5 grams   Fat: 11. 5 grams

TIME-SAVING TIP

Eggs that are a week or two old peel much more quickly and easily than fresh eggs, so this is a great way to use your old eggs.

Crab Rangoon Dip

NUT-FREE   SOY-FREE

Prep time: 5 minutes   **Cook time:** 25 minutes

Crab rangoon is a popular appetizer in Chinese restaurants. The crab puffs are made from fried wontons wrapped around a filling of cream cheese, crab, and scallions. This dip gives you the same flavor without the deep-frying. Serve it with the Baked Corn Tortilla Chips (page 118).

4 ounces cream cheese, at room temperature

$\frac{1}{2}$ cup Low-FODMAP Mayonnaise (page 224)

1 teaspoon Worcestershire sauce

$\frac{1}{4}$ teaspoon cayenne pepper

8 ounces lump crabmeat, drained and flaked

4 scallions (green part only), minced

1. Preheat the oven to 350°F.

2. In a food processor or stand mixer (or with a hand mixer), blend the cream cheese, mayonnaise, Worcestershire sauce, and cayenne until combined. Scrape into a medium bowl. Carefully fold in the crab and scallion greens. Spread the mixture into a 9-inch pie plate.

3. Bake until the dip is hot and bubbly, about 25 minutes. Serve hot.

Serves 4 / **Per Serving**   Calories: 278   Protein: 14 grams
Sugar: 2.5 grams   Fat: 21 grams

Sweet 'n' Spicy Pecans

VEGETARIAN   SOY-FREE

Prep time: 5 minutes   **Cook time:** 10 minutes

While these sweet and spicy pecans are delicious by themselves, they are also tasty on top of a salad. The nuts will keep well in a tightly sealed container for up to 2 weeks. If you like, you can replace the pecans with walnuts.

$\frac{1}{4}$ teaspoon sea salt

$\frac{1}{4}$ teaspoon ground cumin

$\frac{1}{4}$ teaspoon cayenne pepper

$\frac{1}{4}$ teaspoon ground allspice

$\frac{1}{4}$ teaspoon ground cinnamon

8 ounces pecan halves

2 tablespoons unsalted butter

2 tablespoons freshly squeezed orange juice

1 tablespoon dark brown sugar

1. In a small bowl, combine the sea salt, cumin, cayenne, allspice, and cinnamon. Set aside.

2. In a large nonstick skillet over medium heat, cook the nuts, stirring frequently, until they are brown and fragrant, about 4 minutes.

3. Add the butter and allow it to melt and coat the nuts, stirring constantly. Stir in the spices. Add the orange juice and brown sugar. Stirring constantly, allow the spice and juice mixture to thicken and coat the nuts.

4. Remove the nut mixture from the skillet and transfer to a sheet of parchment. Allow to cool completely.

Serves 4 / Per Serving   Calories: 459   Protein: 6 grams
Sugar: 5 grams   Fat: 46 grams

Fresh Salsa

NUT-FREE   VEGETARIAN   VEGAN   PALEO-FRIENDLY   DAIRY-FREE   SOY-FREE

Prep time: 10 minutes, plus 20 minutes resting time   **Cook time:** None

Commercially prepared salsa contains onions and garlic. This low-FODMAP version uses garlic oil and scallion greens to replace those flavors. This is an uncooked salsa, so it needs to be used within about 4 days of making it. Keep it tightly sealed in the refrigerator until you are ready to use it.

4 heirloom or beefsteak tomatoes, chopped

8 scallions (green part only), minced

$1/4$ cup chopped fresh cilantro

2 tablespoons chopped fresh chives

1 jalapeño pepper, seeded and minced

Juice of 1 lime

1 tablespoon Garlic Oil (page 220)

$1/2$ teaspoon sea salt

$1/2$ teaspoon freshly ground black pepper

Pinch cayenne pepper

In a medium bowl, toss together the tomatoes, scallions, cilantro, chives, jalapeño, lime juice, garlic oil, salt, black pepper, and cayenne until well mixed. Allow the salsa to rest for 20 minutes before serving to blend the flavors.

Serves 4 / **Per Serving**   Calories: 63   Protein: 2 grams
Sugar: 4 grams   Fat: 4 grams

Cheese Quesadilla

NUT-FREE   VEGETARIAN   SOY-FREE

Prep time: 5 minutes   **Cook time:** 5 minutes

Quesadillas are very easy to make, so you can have a satisfying snack in less than 10 minutes. While this is a basic cheese quesadilla, you can add other ingredients such as shredded chicken or low-FODMAP vegetables. Serve it with Fresh Salsa (page 128).

  2 (6-inch) corn tortillas
  1 tablespoon Garlic Oil (page 220)
  1 ounce shredded cheddar cheese

1. Preheat a 10-inch skillet over medium-high heat.

2. Brush one corn tortilla with the garlic oil and place it, oiled-side down, in the hot skillet. Top the tortilla with the cheese. Brush the second tortilla with garlic oil and place it on top of the cheese, with the oiled side up.

3. Allow the quesadilla to cook until it begins to brown on the bottom, about 2 minutes. Carefully flip the quesadilla. Allow it to continue cooking until the cheese melts, 2 to 4 more minutes. Cut into wedges and serve.

Serves 1 / **Per Serving**   Calories: 339   Protein: 10 grams
Sugar: 1 gram   Fat: 24 grams

Vegetarian Dinners

Carrot Ginger Soup

NUT-FREE   VEGETARIAN   VEGAN   DAIRY-FREE   SOY-FREE

Prep time: 10 minutes   **Cook time:** 30 minutes

This delicious soup is spiced with ginger and hot pepper flakes, so it has a little bit of heat. The soup is pureed in a food processor or blender before serving. When pureeing hot soup, be sure to protect your hand with a folded towel and regularly remove the food processor's chute to allow steam to escape. (If using a blender, hold the lid down with a towel to prevent it from being forced off.)

20 large carrots, peeled and diced
2 medium celery stalks, diced
1 (1-inch) knob ginger, peeled and grated
½ teaspoon red pepper flakes
5 cups Vegetable Stock (page 99)
¼ teaspoon cayenne pepper
¼ cup unsweetened rice milk
Sea salt
Freshly ground black pepper

1. Combine the carrots, celery, ginger, red pepper flakes , and cayenne pepper in a large pot. Add the vegetable stock and bring to a boil over high heat.

2. Reduce the heat to medium, cover, and simmer until the vegetables are very soft, about 25 minutes.

3. Pour the soup into the bowl of a large food processor or blender, along with the rice milk. If your blender or food processor isn't large enough, you may work in batches.

4. Puree the soup until it is smooth. Taste and season with salt and pepper. Serve hot.

Serves 4 / Per Serving   Calories: 199   Protein: 10 grams
Sugar: 18 grams   Fat: 3 grams

African Peanut Soup

VEGETARIAN   VEGAN   DAIRY-FREE   SOY-FREE

Prep time: 10 minutes   **Cook time:** 25 minutes

This spiced African soup can be made creamy or crunchy, depending on the type of peanut butter you choose. With hot chile peppers, a dash of cayenne, and a blend of spices, it is a warm and comforting soup that's perfect for a cold winter evening. If you are concerned by the high amount of fat, use light coconut milk.

3 tablespoons Garlic Oil (page 220)

2 medium celery stalks, diced

6 scallions (green part only), minced

1 tablespoon peeled grated ginger

1 hot chile pepper, seeded and diced

4 cups Vegetable Stock (page 99)

1 (15-ounce) can coconut milk

2 sweet potatoes, peeled and cut into $\frac{1}{2}$-inch pieces

1 tomato, seeded and chopped

$\frac{1}{8}$ teaspoon ground allspice

$\frac{1}{8}$ teaspoon ground cinnamon

$\frac{1}{2}$ cup peanut butter

Sea salt

Freshly ground black pepper

Chopped peanuts, for garnish (optional)

Chopped fresh cilantro, for garnish (optional)

1. In a large pot, heat the garlic oil over medium-high heat until it shimmers. Add the celery, scallion greens, ginger, and chile pepper. Cook, stirring occasionally, until the vegetables soften, about 4 minutes.

2. Add the vegetable stock, coconut milk, sweet potatoes, tomato, allspice, and cinnamon. Cook, stirring occasionally, until the potatoes soften, about 15 minutes. ➤

African Peanut Soup continued

3. Place 1 cup of the hot soup in a medium-sized bowl, and stir in the peanut butter until the peanut butter melts and combines with the liquid.

4. Return the peanut butter mixture to the pot and stir to combine. Cook, stirring frequently, for an additional 5 minutes. Season with salt and pepper.

5. Serve hot, garnished with peanuts and chopped cilantro, if desired.

Serves 4 / **Per Serving** Calories: 714 Protein: 18 grams
Sugar: 10 grams   Fat: 53 grams

Sweet and Sour Tofu

NUT-FREE   VEGETARIAN   VEGAN   DAIRY-FREE

Prep time: 10 minutes   **Cook time:** 20 minutes

Tofu gets an Asian twist in this stir-fry. The recipe calls for pineapple packed in pineapple juice, which, in less than $\frac{1}{2}$-cup servings, falls within the low-FODMAP guidelines. Serve the sweet and sour tofu on a bed of white rice or rice noodles.

1 (14-ounce) package extra-firm tofu

$\frac{3}{4}$ cup canned pineapple packed in juice

3 tablespoons rice wine vinegar

2 tablespoons gluten-free soy sauce

1 tablespoon brown sugar

2 teaspoons cornstarch

2 tablespoons Garlic Oil (page 220)

1 large green bell pepper, seeded and chopped

1 tablespoon peeled grated ginger

1. Place the tofu in a colander over a bowl, and allow it to drain for at least 30 minutes. Cut the tofu into $\frac{1}{2}$-inch cubes and place in a medium bowl.

2. Drain the pineapple, reserving $\frac{1}{4}$ cup of the juice. In a small bowl, whisk the pineapple juice, rice wine vinegar, soy sauce, and brown sugar, until well mixed.

3. Toss 3 tablespoons of the pineapple juice mixture with the tofu.

4. Whisk the cornstarch into the remaining pineapple juice mixture.

5. Heat 1 tablespoon of the garlic oil in a large sauté pan or wok over medium-high heat until it shimmers. Remove the tofu chunks from the marinade and put them in the hot oil. Cook, stirring occasionally, until brown, about 8 minutes. Remove the tofu from the pan and set aside on a platter.   ➤

Sweet and Sour Tofu continued

6. Add the remaining 1 tablespoon garlic oil to the pan and heat until it shimmers. Add the green bell pepper and ginger. Cook until the vegetables begin to soften, about 4 minutes.

7. Add the pineapple juice–cornstarch mixture to the pan, and cook, stirring constantly, until it thickens, about 2 minutes.

8. Add the pineapple chunks and reserved tofu and cook until heated through, 2 to 3 minutes. Serve.

Serves 4 / **Per Serving**   Calories: 169   Protein: 12 grams
Sugar: 10 grams   Fat: 6 grams

Gluten-Free Penne with Basil-Walnut Pesto

VEGETARIAN SOY-FREE

Prep time: 5 minutes   **Cook time:** 10 minutes

Traditional pesto is a mixture of pine nuts, basil, Parmesan cheese, garlic, and olive oil. This pesto replaces the garlic with garlic oil and the pine nuts with walnuts. If you'd prefer a more traditional pesto, you can use an equal amount of pine nuts in place of the walnuts.

1 pound gluten-free penne pasta

2 cups tightly packed basil leaves

$\frac{1}{2}$ cup chopped walnuts

$\frac{1}{2}$ cup grated Parmesan cheese

$\frac{1}{3}$ cup Garlic Oil (page 220)

1. Bring a large pot of water to a boil over high heat. Add the penne and cook according to the package instructions until al dente, 9 to 11 minutes.

2. Meanwhile, pulse the basil, walnuts, Parmesan, and garlic oil in a food processor to finely chop and blend the ingredients. Do not puree.

3. When the pasta is done, drain it in a colander. Toss the hot pasta with the pesto. Serve immediately.

Serves 4 / **Per Serving**   Calories: 727   Protein: 22 grams
Sugar: 2 grams   Fat: 33 grams

Gluten-Free Angel Hair Pasta with Vegetable Marinara

NUT-FREE   VEGETARIAN   VEGAN   DAIRY-FREE   SOY-FREE

Prep time: 15 minutes   **Cook time:** 20 minutes

Many jarred marinara sauces are high in FODMAPs and contain added high-fructose corn syrup (HFCS). This easy marinara is low in FODMAPs and uses fresh, healthy vegetables. Although this recipe calls for angel hair pasta, you can choose any shape you wish. Serve it topped with grated Parmesan cheese.

12 ounces gluten-free angel hair pasta

3 tablespoons Garlic Oil (page 220)

6 scallions (green part only), minced

2 carrots, peeled and thinly sliced

1 red bell pepper, seeded and diced

1 green bell pepper, seeded and diced

1 (28-ounce) can crushed tomatoes

1 teaspoon dried oregano

1 teaspoon dried Italian seasoning

Sea salt

Freshly ground black pepper

1. Bring a large pot of water to a boil, and cook the pasta according to the package directions until al dente, 3 to 9 minutes. Drain the pasta.

2. Meanwhile, in a large pot, heat the garlic oil over medium-high heat until it shimmers. Add the scallion greens, carrots, and bell peppers and cook until soft, about 5 minutes. Add the crushed tomatoes, oregano, and Italian seasoning. Simmer until warmed through, about 5 minutes.

3. Season the sauce with sea salt and pepper, and toss with the pasta. Serve.

Serves 4 / **Per Serving**   Calories: 410   Protein: 10 grams
Sugar: 11 grams   Fat: 1 gram

Enchiladas with Olives and Cheddar

NUT-FREE   VEGETARIAN   SOY-FREE

Prep time: 10 minutes   **Cook time:** 30 minutes

These enchiladas have a flavorful filling made from cheese, olives, and jalapeños. The enchilada sauce comes together quickly, because aromatic ingredients are pulsed together in a food processor into a very fine dice and then cooked quickly in olive oil. If you don't have a food processor, you can finely mince the vegetables with a knife. Be sure to choose a tomato sauce and a chili powder that do not have added garlic or onion.

FOR THE ENCHILADA SAUCE

6 scallions (green part only)

1 jalapeño pepper, seeded

1 tablespoon chopped chives

3 tablespoons Garlic Oil (page 220)

1 (8-ounce) can tomato sauce

3 tablespoons chili powder

$\frac{1}{2}$ teaspoon dried oregano

$\frac{1}{2}$ teaspoon ground cumin

$\frac{1}{2}$ teaspoon sea salt

$\frac{1}{4}$ teaspoon cayenne pepper

FOR THE ENCHILADAS

2 (4-ounce) cans chopped black olives, drained

1 (4-ounce) can diced jalapeño peppers, drained

8 ounces cheddar cheese, grated

8 (6-inch) corn tortillas   ➤

Enchiladas with Olives and Cheddar continued

TO MAKE THE ENCHILADA SAUCE

1. Place the scallion greens, fresh jalapeño, and chives in a food processor, and pulse briefly to mince and combine the vegetables.

2. In a medium-sized saucepan, heat the garlic oil over medium-high heat until it shimmers. Add the vegetables from the food processor and cook until very fragrant, about 2 minutes. Add the tomato sauce, chili powder, oregano, cumin, salt, and cayenne. Simmer for 5 minutes to integrate the flavors. Pour the enchilada sauce into a shallow dish.

TO MAKE THE ENCHILADAS

1. Preheat the oven to 350°F.

2. In a small bowl, combine the olives, canned jalapeños, and 6 ounces of the cheese.

3. Dip each corn tortilla in the enchilada sauce. Spoon an equal portion of the cheese mixture down the center of each tortilla and roll them up. Place the rolled enchiladas in a 9-by-13-inch baking pan. Pour the remaining sauce over the top of the enchiladas. Sprinkle with the remaining 2 ounces cheese.

4. Bake until warm and bubbly, about 20 minutes. Serve.

Serves 4 / **Per Serving** Calories: 506 Protein: 18 grams
Sugar: 2 grams Fat: 36 grams

INGREDIENT VARIATION

If you wish, you can make these cheese enchiladas by leaving out the olives and chopped jalapeños. You can also add 2 cups diced tofu to the filling to up the protein content.

Grilled Tofu Burgers with Lemon and Basil

NUT-FREE   VEGETARIAN   DAIRY-FREE

Prep time: 10 minutes, plus 1 hour marinating time   **Cook time:** 6 minutes

Marinated tofu is the star in these burgers, which are delicious right off the grill. If you don't have a grill, you can sauté the burgers in a nonstick sauté pan over medium-high heat. You can usually find gluten-free hamburger buns at the grocery store in either the bread aisle or the freezer section; if not, you can always use toasted gluten-free sandwich bread.

2 tablespoons Garlic Oil (page 220)

2 tablespoons Dijon mustard

$\frac{1}{4}$ cup freshly squeezed lemon juice

Zest of $\frac{1}{2}$ lemon, finely grated

$\frac{1}{3}$ cup finely chopped fresh basil

$\frac{1}{4}$ teaspoon sea salt

$\frac{1}{4}$ teaspoon freshly ground black pepper

1 pound extra-firm tofu, drained

4 gluten-free hamburger buns

8 tablespoons Garlic Mayonnaise (page 224)

Arugula leaves, for serving

1. In a small bowl, whisk together the garlic oil, Dijon mustard, lemon juice, lemon zest, basil, sea salt, and pepper.

2. Slice the tofu lengthwise into four slices. Marinate the tofu in the garlic oil mixture for 1 hour.

3. Heat the grill to high. Lightly brush the grate with oil.

4. Grill the tofu over direct heat for 3 minutes per side.   ➤

Grilled Tofu Burgers with Lemon and Basil continued

5. Spread each hamburger bun with 2 tablespoons garlic mayonnaise.

6. Place the grilled tofu on the buns and top with arugula. Serve.

....

Serves 4 / **Per Serving**   Calories: 454   Protein: 15 grams
Sugar: 7 grams   Fat: 27 grams

Grilled Eggplant with Tomato and Basil Salad

NUT-FREE   VEGETARIAN   SOY-FREE

Prep time: 15 minutes, plus 1 hour resting time   **Cook time:** 8 minutes

Salting eggplant and allowing it to sit before you cook it draws out the water in the eggplant. This removes the bitterness and allows the eggplant to grill quickly. Wipe the salt off the eggplant, and pat it dry thoroughly with paper towels before putting it on the grill. You can also cook the eggplant in a sauté pan over medium-high heat for about 4 minutes per side if you don't have a grill.

1 large eggplant, peeled and sliced crosswise into $1/4$-inch-thick slices
Sea salt
2 large heirloom or beefsteak tomatoes, seeded and diced
8 ounces mozzarella, cubed
$1/2$ cup Garlic-Basil Vinaigrette (page 221)
Freshly ground black pepper

1. Line a baking sheet with paper towels, and place the eggplant slices in a single layer on the paper towels. Sprinkle the eggplant with salt. Allow the salted eggplant to sit for 1 hour.

2. Combine the tomatoes, mozzarella, and vinaigrette in a medium bowl. Set it aside to marinate while the eggplant rests.

3. Preheat the grill to high. Lightly brush the grate with oil.

4. Wipe the salt away from the eggplant and pat dry with paper towels.

5. Grill the eggplant slices over direct heat for 4 minutes per side.

6. Serve the eggplant warm, topped with the tomato salad. Season with pepper.

Serves 4 / Per Serving   Calories: 339   Protein: 17 grams
Sugar: 5 grams   Fat: 25 grams

Lentil and Vegetable Sloppy Joes

NUT-FREE   VEGETARIAN   VEGAN   DAIRY-FREE

Prep time: 15 minutes   **Cook time:** 20 minutes

Sloppy joes don't need meat to be delicious. These are loaded with finely diced, flavorful vegetables, and lentils replace the meat. According to Monash University, canned lentils are low-FODMAP if you limit yourself to $\frac{1}{2}$ cup. Do not use dried lentils in this recipe.

2 tablespoons Garlic Oil (page 220)
6 scallions (green part only), diced
1 green bell pepper, seeded and diced
1 red bell pepper, seeded and diced
1 zucchini, seeded and diced
2 cups canned lentils, drained and rinsed
1 (15-ounce) can tomato sauce
1 tablespoon red wine vinegar
1 tablespoon gluten-free soy sauce
1 tablespoon Worcestershire sauce
$\frac{1}{4}$ cup dark brown sugar
$\frac{1}{4}$ teaspoon cayenne pepper
Sea salt
Freshly ground black pepper
4 gluten-free hamburger buns

1. In a large sauté pan, heat the garlic oil over medium-high heat until it shimmers. Add the scallions, bell peppers, and zucchini. Cook until the vegetables soften and begin to brown, about 5 minutes.

2. Add the lentils, tomato sauce, red wine vinegar, soy sauce, Worcestershire sauce, brown sugar, and cayenne. Stirring constantly, simmer the sauce until the lentils and vegetables are soft, about 10 minutes more. Season with sea salt and pepper.

3. Serve on gluten-free hamburger buns.

Serves 4 / **Per Serving** Calories: 681 Protein: 32 grams
Sugar: 22 grams Fat: 13 grams

INGREDIENT TIP

When selecting a tomato sauce, remember to choose one that does not have onion or garlic added to it.

Fried Rice with Tofu and Water Chestnuts

NUT-FREE   VEGETARIAN   DAIRY-FREE

Prep time: 10 minutes   **Cook time:** 15 minutes

With tofu and eggs, this fried rice is hearty enough to be a main course. To save time, purchase precooked rice, which can be found in the freezer or rice section of the grocery store. It's also a great way to use leftover rice and vegetables.

4 tablespoons Garlic Oil (page 220)

8 ounces extra-firm tofu, diced

1 carrot, peeled and diced

6 scallions (green part only), chopped

1 tablespoon peeled grated ginger

1 (8-ounce) can sliced water chestnuts, drained and rinsed

4 large eggs, beaten

$\frac{1}{4}$ cup gluten-free soy sauce

2 cups cooked white rice

1. In a large sauté pan or wok, heat the garlic oil over medium-high heat until it shimmers. Add the tofu, carrot, scallion greens, ginger, and water chestnuts and cook until the carrots soften, about 5 minutes.

2. Add the eggs and cook, stirring constantly, until the eggs are set, about 4 minutes. Break up the eggs with a spoon. Add the soy sauce and rice.

3. Cook, stirring constantly, until the rice is hot, about 4 minutes. Serve immediately.

Serves 4 / **Per Serving**   Calories: 619   Protein: 20 grams
Sugar: 2 grams   Fat: 21 grams

8

Fish and Seafood Dinners

Steamed Clams

Prep time: 10 minutes   **Cook time:** 15 minutes

Cook and serve these clams in the shell. The clams can be served in a bowl with the broth and a crusty gluten-free bread for dipping, or you can spoon the broth and clams over a bed of white rice.

2 tablespoons Garlic Oil (page 220)
½ cup chopped fennel
6 scallions (green part only), chopped
4 pounds clams, in shells, washed
2 cups dry white wine
Juice of 2 lemons
Freshly ground black pepper

1. In a large pot, heat the garlic oil over medium-high heat until it shimmers. Add the fennel and scallion greens. Cook, stirring frequently, until the vegetables are soft, about 5 minutes.

2. Add the clams, white wine, lemon juice, and pepper.

3. Bring to a simmer. Cover and simmer until all of the clamshells pop open, about 10 minutes. Serve with the broth.

Serves 4 / **Per Serving**   Calories: 332   Protein: 3 grams
Sugar: 16 grams   Fat: 1 gram

> **WARNING**
>
> Discard any clams that do not open during the steaming process, as they may have gone bad. Do not eat them.

Lemon Pepper Cod with Braised Fennel

Prep time: 10 minutes   **Cook time:** 25 minutes

Fennel has a light licorice flavor that pairs well with fish and seafood. When cooking with fennel, use the bulb at the bottom and discard the stalks. The lemon zest should contain as little of the white pith as possible to prevent bitterness.

4 (4-ounce) cod fillets

Freshly ground black pepper

3 tablespoons olive oil

Juice and grated zest of 1 lemon

2 fennel bulbs, cut in $\frac{1}{2}$-inch slices through the core

$\frac{3}{4}$ cup Vegetable Stock (page 99)

1 tomato, seeded and finely chopped

2 tablespoons capers, drained

1. Season the cod fillets liberally with pepper.

2. In a large sauté pan, heat 2 tablespoons of the olive oil over medium-high heat until it shimmers. Add the cod to the pan. Sprinkle half of the lemon juice over the top. Cook for 4 minutes without moving the cod.

3. Flip the cod. Sprinkle the remaining lemon juice over the top. Cook until the cod flakes easily, about 4 more minutes. Remove the cod from the pan and set aside, tented with foil.

4. Add the remaining 1 tablespoon olive oil to the pan and heat until it shimmers. Cook the fennel, turning the slices once, for 4 minutes. Reduce the heat to low. Add the vegetable stock and lemon zest. Cover and cook until the fennel is tender, about 10 minutes.   ➤

Lemon Pepper Cod with Braised Fennel continued

5. Place the fennel on plates. Place the cod on top of the fennel. Spoon the braising liquid over the cod, and top with tomatoes and capers. Serve.

....

Serves 4 / **Per Serving**   Calories: 253   Protein: 28 grams
Sugar: 0 grams   Fat: 12 grams

INGREDIENT TIP

Reserve the fennel fronds (the feathery parts on the stalks of the fennel). Chop them finely and sprinkle over the top of the dish as a garnish.

Scallops with White Wine Tarragon Sauce

NUT-FREE   SOY-FREE

Prep time: 10 minutes   **Cook time:** 10 minutes

For best results, use large fresh sea scallops for this recipe. The scallops are lightly sweet, and the tarragon butter sauce adds richness to the meal. Serve on a bed of gluten-free angel hair pasta with steamed vegetables on the side.

16 large sea scallops, washed and patted dry with paper towels

Sea salt

Freshly ground black pepper

2 tablespoons olive oil

1 cup dry white wine

Juice of 1 lemon

2 tablespoons chopped fresh chives

2 tablespoons chopped fresh tarragon

$\frac{1}{2}$ cup cold unsalted butter, cut into $\frac{1}{2}$-inch cubes

1. Season the scallops with salt and pepper.

2. In a large sauté pan over medium-high heat, heat the oil until it shimmers. Add the scallops in a single layer, making sure not to crowd the pan. Cook in batches if you have to. Cook the scallops without moving them until they begin to brown, about 4 minutes.

3. Flip the scallops and cook on the other side until they brown, 3 to 4 minutes. Remove the scallops from the pan and set aside on a platter.

4. Add the wine and lemon juice to the pan, scraping up any browned bits from the bottom of the pan. Reduce the heat to medium-low.

5. Add the chives and tarragon. Simmer until the liquid is reduced to 2 tablespoons, 3 to 4 minutes. ➤

Scallops with White Wine Tarragon Sauce continued

6. Add the butter to the pan, one cube at a time, whisking constantly to emulsify. When the butter is all incorporated, return the scallops to the pan. Turn them once to coat with sauce.

7. Serve the scallops with the sauce spooned over the top.

....

Serves 4 / **Per Serving**   Calories: 391   Protein: 21 grams
Sugar: 2 grams   Fat: 31 grams

INGREDIENT TIP

Choose sea scallops that are firm to the touch. Raw scallops should smell sweet, not fishy.

Shrimp Cakes with Lime Chili Aioli

NUT-FREE   DAIRY-FREE   SOY-FREE

Prep time: 20 minutes   **Cook time:** 15 minutes

Serve these shrimp cakes with roasted potatoes or on a bed of rice with the aioli spooned over the top, and a refreshing low-FODMAP fruit salad on the side. If you prefer, you can replace the shrimp with another type of seafood, such as lump crabmeat or flaked halibut.

1 pound large raw shrimp, peeled, deveined, and rinsed

1 large egg, beaten

2 scallions (green part only), diced

2 tablespoons freshly squeezed lemon juice

1 tablespoon Dijon mustard

$3/4$ teaspoon cayenne pepper

2 cups gluten-free bread crumbs

$1/8$ teaspoon sea salt

1 cup Low-FODMAP Mayonnaise (page 224)

Juice and grated zest of 1 lime

$1/2$ teaspoon paprika

2 tablespoons olive oil

1. In the bowl of a food processor, pulse the shrimp to coarsely chop it.

2. Add the egg, scallion greens, lemon juice, Dijon mustard, and $1/4$ teaspoon of the cayenne. Pulse briefly to combine. Add 1 cup of the bread crumbs and pulse briefly to combine. ➤

Shrimp Cakes with Lime Chili Aioli continued

3. Form the mixture into 8 cakes. Roll the cakes in the remaining 1 cup bread crumbs. Place on a parchment-lined baking sheet and refrigerate for 10 minutes.

4. While the shrimp cakes rest, in a small bowl whisk together the mayonnaise, lime juice, lime zest, paprika, remaining $1/2$ teaspoon cayenne, and sea salt. Set aside.

5. In a large nonstick pan, heat the oil over medium-high heat until it shimmers. Working in batches, fry the cakes until they are golden brown on both sides, about 4 minutes per side. Serve the cakes topped with the aioli.

Serves 4 / **Per Serving** Calories: 660 Protein: 35 grams
Sugar: 8 grams Fat: 32 grams

INGREDIENT TIP

You can make gluten-free bread crumbs by removing the crusts from stale gluten-free sandwich bread and pulsing it in the food processor until it resembles coarse sand. In addition, many grocery stores now sell gluten-free breadcrumbs, which will save time.

Grilled Shrimp Tacos with Cilantro

NUT-FREE   SOY-FREE

Prep time: 15 minutes   **Cook time:** 20 minutes

Shrimp marinated in lime juice and garlic oil serves as the focal point for these tacos. To add a smokier flavor, warm the corn tortillas on the grill until they get grill marks. If you don't have a grill, you can also sauté the shrimp and scallion greens in a large sauté pan over medium-high heat until they turn pink, about 5 minutes. Heat the warm corn tortillas in a 350°F oven, wrapped in foil, for 10 minutes. Top with Fresh Salsa (page 128).

2 tablespoons Garlic Oil (page 220)

Juice of 1 lime

1/4 teaspoon cayenne pepper

1 pound large raw shrimp, peeled, deveined, and rinsed

8 scallions

8 (6-inch) corn tortillas

4 ounces cheddar cheese, shredded

1/4 cup chopped fresh cilantro

1. In a medium bowl, whisk together the garlic oil, lime juice, and cayenne. Toss with the shrimp and allow it to sit for 10 minutes.

2. Heat the grill to medium and lightly grease it. Thread the shrimp on skewers and place them on the grill. Cook the shrimp until it is pink, about 5 minutes per side.

3. Place the scallions on the grill and cook, turning occasionally, until they are lightly charred, about 3 minutes per side. Cut the white part off the scallions and discard it. Cut the scallion greens in half crosswise.   ➤

Grilled Shrimp Tacos with Cilantro continued

4. Grill the tortillas on the grill, turning occasionally, about 3 minutes per side.

5. To assemble, wrap the shrimp, scallion greens, cheddar cheese, and cilantro in the warm corn tortillas. Serve.

....

Serves 4 / **Per Serving** Calories: 424 Protein: 36 grams
Sugar: 4 grams Fat: 20 grams

Shrimp Scampi

NUT-FREE   PALEO-FRIENDLY   DAIRY-FREE   SOY-FREE

Prep time: 15 minutes   **Cook time:** 6 minutes

Shrimp scampi is a traditional Italian dish with lots of garlic. Since garlic contains FODMAPs, this recipe uses garlic oil. Serve the scampi on a bed of gluten-free spaghetti with the sauce spooned over the top.

$1\frac{1}{2}$ pounds jumbo raw shrimp, peeled and deveined

Sea salt

Freshly ground black pepper

2 tablespoons Garlic Oil (page 220)

$\frac{1}{4}$ cup dry white wine

1 tablespoon freshly squeezed lemon juice

1 tablespoon finely chopped flat-leaf parsley

$\frac{1}{2}$ teaspoon finely grated fresh lemon zest

1. Season the shrimp with salt and pepper.

2. In a large sauté pan over medium-high heat, heat the garlic oil until it shimmers. Add the shrimp. Allow the shrimp to sit without stirring for 2 minutes. Turn the shrimp over and cook for 2 minutes on the other side.

3. Add the wine and lemon juice, scraping up any browned bits from the bottom of the pan. Bring to a simmer. Stir in the parsley and lemon zest. Serve.

Serves 4 / Per Serving Calories: 194   Protein: 30 grams
Sugar: 3 grams   Fat: 7 grams

Halibut with Lemon-Basil Beurre Blanc and Braised Endive

NUT-FREE SOY-FREE

Prep time: 15 minutes   **Cook time:** 20 minutes

Beurre blanc is a traditional French sauce. To make it, you reduce an acidic liquid and then incorporate very cold unsalted butter one small piece at a time to create an emulsion. Traditional beurre blanc calls for shallots, which contain FODMAPs, so in this recipe, you will use chives instead, straining them out before final presentation.

FOR THE ENDIVE

2 tablespoons unsalted butter

4 heads Belgian endive, halved lengthwise

1 cup Vegetable Stock (page 99)

1 teaspoon freshly squeezed lemon juice

FOR THE HALIBUT

2 tablespoons olive oil

Sea salt

Freshly ground black pepper

1 (16-ounce) halibut fillet, cut crosswise into 4 pieces

$1/2$ cup dry white wine

2 teaspoons freshly squeezed lemon juice

1 tablespoon finely chopped fresh chives

4 ounces cold butter, cut into $1/2$-inch cubes

2 tablespoons finely chopped fresh basil

TO MAKE THE ENDIVE

1. In a large sauté pan, heat the butter over medium-high heat until it bubbles. Add the endive, cut-side down, and cook without moving until it browns slightly, about 4 minutes.

2. Add the vegetable stock and lemon juice, and bring to a simmer. Reduce the heat to medium. Cook the endive, uncovered, turning occasionally, until it can be pierced with a fork, about 10 minutes.

3. Increase the heat to medium-high and simmer until the liquid has evaporated, about 2 minutes. Remove from the heat.

TO MAKE THE HALIBUT

1. Heat the oil in a large sauté pan over medium-high heat until it shimmers. Season the halibut with salt and pepper, and put it in the pan, skin-side down. Cook for 5 minutes.

2. Flip the halibut and cook it on the other side for 5 minutes. Remove the halibut from the pan, and set it aside, tented with foil to keep it warm.

3. Add the wine, lemon juice, and chives to the pan, scraping up any browned bits from the bottom of the pan. Bring to a simmer and reduce the heat to medium-low. Simmer until the liquid reduces to about 2 tablespoons.

4. Working with one piece at a time, whisk in the butter, stirring constantly to emulsify the sauce. When the butter is completely incorporated, strain the sauce through a fine-mesh sieve into a small bowl. Whisk in the basil.

5. Serve the sauce spooned over the halibut, with the braised endive on the side.

Serves 4 / **Per Serving**   Calories: 608   Protein: 38 grams
Sugar: 2 grams   Fat: 42 grams

Grill-Poached Halibut with Lemon and Dill

NUT-FREE   SOY-FREE

Prep time: 10 minutes   **Cook time:** 10 minutes

In this recipe, halibut is poached in butter, white wine, lemon, and dill. Instead of poaching it on the stove top, however, you poach it on the grill in aluminum foil packets. This cooking method requires very little attention and yields tender halibut. If you don't have a grill, you can place the packets in a 450°F oven for 8 to 10 minutes. Serve with a crisp green salad for a light summer meal.

1 (16-ounce) halibut fillet, cut crosswise into 4 pieces
Sea salt
Freshly ground black pepper
4 large dill sprigs, finely chopped
2 lemons, sliced
½ cup unsalted butter, cut into 8 pats
1 cup dry white wine

1. Heat the grill to medium-high. Lightly oil the grate.

2. Place each halibut piece on a sheet of aluminum foil large enough to fold over and enclose the fish. Season the halibut liberally with salt and pepper. Sprinkle the dill on top of the halibut. Place the lemon slices on top of the dill. Place the butter pats on top of the lemon slices. Fold up the sides of each sheet of foil. Carefully pour ¼ cup of the wine into each packet. Seal the packets by folding the foil over the top and crimping the edges to seal.

3. Place the foil packets on the preheated grill. Grill until the fish is cooked through, 8 to 10 minutes. Serve.

Serves 4 / **Per Serving**   Calories: 411   Protein: 30 grams
Sugar: 0 grams   Fat: 26 grams

Maple-Soy Glazed Salmon

Prep time: 10 minutes   **Cook time:** 10 minutes

Salmon is high in omega-3 fatty acids, so this is a very healthy entrée. This salmon is grilled with a simple glaze made from gluten-free soy sauce and pure maple syrup. If you don't have a grill, you can bake the salmon on a rimmed baking sheet in a 450°F oven for 8 to 10 minutes. Serve the salmon with steamed vegetables and a salad.

$\frac{1}{4}$ cup pure maple syrup

$\frac{1}{4}$ cup gluten-free soy sauce

1 (16-ounce) salmon fillet, cut crosswise into 4 pieces

1. Whisk together the syrup and soy sauce in a shallow dish.

2. Place the salmon in the marinade, flesh-side down. Marinate for 10 minutes.

3. Preheat the grill on medium high and lightly oil the grate. Place the salmon on the grill, skin-side down, and brush the top with marinade. Cook for 3 minutes.

4. Flip the salmon and cook to form grill marks, about 4 minutes.

5. Turn the salmon over again. Close the grill lid and cook until the salmon is opaque, about 3 more minutes. Serve.

Serves 4 / **Per Serving**   Calories: 210   Protein: 23 grams
Sugar: 12 grams   Fat: 7 grams

Hearty Clam Chowder with Fennel

NUT-FREE   SOY-FREE

Prep time: 15 minutes   **Cook time:** 25 minutes

This smoky clam chowder uses leek tops in place of onions to flavor the chowder. Use the bulb of the fennel, as well as the chopped fronds, to add an anise flavor to the chowder that goes well with clams.

$1/2$ pound pepper bacon, cut into $1/2$-inch pieces

2 carrots, peeled and diced

1 fennel bulb, diced, plus 2 tablespoons chopped fronds

1 leek (green part only), chopped

3 tablespoons gluten-free flour

6 cups Vegetable Stock (page 99)

1 teaspoon dried thyme

3 (6. 5 ounce) cans clams, drained and rinsed

12 baby red potatoes, quartered

$1/4$ cup lactose-free whole milk

$1/4$ teaspoon cayenne pepper

Sea salt

Freshly ground black pepper

1. In a large stockpot, cook the bacon, stirring frequently until the fat renders and the bacon is crisp, about 5 minutes. Remove the bacon from the fat with a slotted spoon and set aside to drain on paper towels.

2. Add the carrots, diced fennel, and leek greens to the bacon fat and cook, stirring occasionally, until the vegetables begin to brown, about 6 minutes. Stir in the flour and cook, stirring constantly, for 3 minutes.

3. Stir in the vegetable stock and dried thyme, scraping up any browned bits from the bottom of the pan. Add the clams and potatoes. Simmer the soup until the potatoes are tender, about 10 minutes.

4. Stir in the milk, reserved bacon, fennel fronds, and cayenne. Season with salt and pepper. Serve.

....

Serves 4 / **Per Serving**   Calories: 853   Protein: 40 grams
Sugar: 10 grams   Fat: 30 grams

Meat and Poultry Dinners

Teriyaki Chicken

NUT-FREE   DAIRY-FREE

Prep time: 10 minutes   **Cook time:** 20 minutes

Teriyaki chicken is a family favorite with its sweet sticky sauce. Unfortunately, commercially prepared teriyaki sauce contains soy sauce, which has wheat. Some teriyaki sauce also contains honey, which is a source of fructose. This recipe comes together quickly with items you probably have in your pantry, so it's a great weeknight meal served on a bed of rice with the sauce spooned over the top.

$3/4$ cup gluten-free soy sauce

$1/4$ cup brown sugar

$1^1/2$ teaspoons peeled grated ginger

4 (4-ounce) boneless, skinless chicken breasts

Freshly ground black pepper

2 tablespoons canola oil

2 scallions (green part only), thinly sliced

1 tablespoon sesame seeds

1. In a small saucepan over medium heat, simmer the soy sauce and brown sugar until the brown sugar dissolves, about 5 minutes. Stir in the ginger. Simmer for another minute, and then remove from the heat and set aside.

2. Place a layer of plastic wrap on a cutting board, and place a chicken breast on top of it. Cover the chicken with another layer of plastic wrap. Gently pound the chicken breast until it reaches $1/2$-inch thickness. Repeat with the remaining chicken breasts. Season the chicken with pepper.

3. In a large skillet or sauté pan, heat the oil over medium-high heat until it shimmers. Place the chicken in the pan in a single layer. Allow the chicken to cook without moving it until it browns, 3 to 4 minutes. Flip the chicken and cook it on the other side, another 4 minutes.

4. Reduce the heat to medium. Pour in the sauce and bring it to a simmer. Simmer for 4 minutes, turning the chicken a few times to coat it with the sauce.

5. Transfer the chicken to a clean cutting board, and slice diagonally into $\frac{1}{2}$-inch slices. Meanwhile, allow the sauce to continue to simmer on the stove top until it thickens, about 3 minutes.

6. Top the chicken with the extra sauce. Sprinkle with the scallion greens and sesame seeds and serve.

....

Serves 4 / **Per Serving**   Calories: 353   Protein: 36 grams
Sugar: 10 grams   Fat: 16 grams

Balsamic Dijon Grilled Chicken Skewers with Mixed Bell Peppers

NUT-FREE   PALEO-FRIENDLY   DAIRY-FREE   SOY-FREE

Prep time: 15 minutes, plus 1 hour for marinating   **Cook time:** 15 minutes

While this recipe calls for Balsamic Dijon Dressing, you can use any of the vinaigrettes found in Chapter 11. If you have time, marinate the chicken for the full 3 hours for the best flavor penetration. If you're running short on time, 1 hour will be adequate to impart flavor. If you don't have a grill, you can bake the skewers on a rimmed baking sheet in a 425°F oven for 8 to 10 minutes.

1 pound boneless, skinless chicken breasts, cut into 1-inch cubes

1 cup Balsamic Dijon Dressing (page 222)

1 green bell pepper, seeded and cut into $1\frac{1}{2}$ inch pieces

1 red bell pepper, seeded and cut into $1\frac{1}{2}$ inch pieces

1 orange bell pepper, seeded and cut into $1\frac{1}{2}$ inch pieces

1. Place the chicken in a large zipper-top plastic bag. Pour in $\frac{3}{4}$ cup of the dressing. Seal the bag and shake it around to distribute the dressing. Place the bag in the refrigerator and allow it to marinate for 1 to 3 hours.

2. Heat the grill to high and lightly brush the grate with oil.

3. Thread the chicken and peppers onto the skewers, alternating the chicken and the three colors of pepper.

4. Grill over direct heat, brushing with the remaining $\frac{1}{4}$ cup dressing frequently. Cook, turning the skewers occasionally, until the juices run clear, about 15 minutes. Serve.

Serves 4 / **Per Serving**   Calories: 404   Protein: 33 grams
Sugar: 4 grams   Fat: 27 grams

INGREDIENT VARIATION

You can vary this recipe in many ways. For example, replace the chicken with cubes of beef, pork, or lamb. Mix with the marinade in the morning, and leave it in the refrigerator all night. You can also use zucchini cut into 1-inch cubes in addition to, or in place of, the peppers.

Chicken Piccata

NUT-FREE   SOY-FREE

Prep time: 10 minutes   **Cook time:** 20 minutes

Piccata is a traditional Italian method of preparing a cut of protein that involves coating the meat with flour, sautéing it, and serving it in a lemony sauce. While veal is the meat most commonly used in Italy for a piccata, this recipe calls for chicken.

4 (4-ounce) boneless, skinless chicken breasts, cut into $1/2$-inch pieces
Sea salt
Freshly ground black pepper
$1/2$ cup gluten-free all-purpose flour
2 tablespoons Garlic Oil (page 220)
1 cup Vegetable Stock (page 99)
$1/2$ lemon, thinly sliced
$1/4$ cup freshly squeezed lemon juice
2 tablespoons capers, rinsed and drained
3 tablespoons cold unsalted butter, cut into $1/2$-inch pieces
2 tablespoons minced fresh flat-leaf parsley

1. Preheat the oven to 200°F.

2. Season the chicken with salt and pepper, and dredge it lightly in the gluten-free flour, tapping the chicken to remove any excess flour.

3. In a large sauté pan or skillet, heat the oil over medium-high heat until it shimmers. Working in batches so you don't crowd the pan, cook the chicken pieces, stirring frequently, until they are golden brown on all sides, about 3 minutes per side.

4. Remove the chicken from the pan with tongs, and place it on an oven-safe platter. Place the platter in the oven to keep warm.

5. Add the vegetable stock to the pan, scraping up any browned bits from the pan. Add the lemon slices and bring to a boil. Allow the sauce to reduce to about ⅔ cups, 5 to 8 minutes, stirring occasionally.

6. Stir in the lemon juice and capers and simmer for an additional 5 minutes. Swirl the butter into the pan, one piece at a time, whisking to emulsify.

7. Pour the sauce over the chicken and garnish with the parsley. Serve.

....

Serves 4 / Per Serving   Calories: 423   Protein: 36 grams
Sugar: 1 gram   Fat: 25 grams

Chicken Carbonara

NUT-FREE   SOY-FREE

Prep time: 10 minutes   **Cook time:** 30 minutes

Carbonara is a traditional Italian pasta with a bacon and egg sauce. This recipe includes chicken for extra protein. You can make the sauce while the spaghetti cooks, and then toss it with the hot, drained spaghetti so it coats every strand.

7 ounces gluten-free spaghetti

8 bacon slices, cut into $\frac{1}{2}$-inch pieces

1 tablespoon Garlic Oil (page 220)

12 ounces boneless, skinless chicken breast, cut into 1-inch pieces

6 scallions (green part only), chopped

3 large eggs

$\frac{1}{4}$ cup lactose-free whole milk

$\frac{1}{2}$ cup grated Parmesan cheese

Freshly ground black pepper

1. Bring a large pot of water to a boil over high heat. Cook the spaghetti according to the package directions until it is al dente, 8 to 12 minutes. Drain the pasta in a colander.

2. In a large sauté pan, cook the bacon over medium-high heat, stirring occasionally, until it is browned and crisp, about 5 minutes.

3. Remove the bacon from the pan with a slotted spoon, and set it aside to drain on paper towels. Remove all but 1 tablespoon of the bacon fat from the pan and return the pan to the heat. Add the garlic oil and heat until it shimmers.

4. Add the chicken to the pan and cook, stirring occasionally, until it is completely browned on all sides, about 3 minutes per side. Remove the chicken from the pan with tongs and set it aside with the bacon.

5. Add the scallion greens to the pan and cook, stirring occasionally, until softened, about 4 minutes.

6. Meanwhile, in a small bowl, whisk together the eggs and milk until very well combined.

7. Add the hot spaghetti, bacon, and chicken to the pan with the scallion greens, and remove the pan from heat.

8. Add the egg-milk mixture to the hot pasta in a thin stream, stirring constantly. Toss with the Parmesan cheese and pepper. Serve.

....

Serves 4 / **Per Serving**   Calories: 650   Protein: 50 grams
Sugar: 1.1 grams   Fat: 31 grams

WARNING

This recipe uses raw eggs, although the hot pasta cooks them slightly without scrambling them. To protect yourself from contamination from raw eggs, use very fresh eggs that are less than a week old or use pasteurized eggs.

TIME-SAVING TIP

Purchase a rotisserie chicken from the deli, remove the skin, and shred the breast meat into the pasta in the final step. This will save you the time involved in cooking the chicken.

Chicken Fingers

NUT-FREE   SOY-FREE

Prep time: 10 minutes   **Cook time:** 30 minutes

One of the things kids love about chicken fingers is the crispy coating. Since traditional chicken fingers contain gluten, commercially prepared versions are out on a low-FODMAP diet. This version uses crumbled tortilla chips, making it a great meal to prepare if you are eating together as a family.

6 cups Baked Corn Tortilla Chips (page 118)
$\frac{1}{2}$ teaspoon sea salt
$\frac{1}{8}$ teaspoon freshly ground black pepper
$\frac{1}{2}$ teaspoon paprika
2 large eggs, slightly beaten
1 pound boneless, skinless chicken breasts, cut into 1-inch strips
$\frac{1}{2}$ cup Ranch Dressing (page 226)

1. Preheat the oven to 450°F. Coat a baking sheet with nonstick cooking spray.

2. Place the corn tortilla chips, sea salt, pepper, and paprika in a food processor, and pulse briefly until the chips are coarsely chopped. If you don't have a food processor, you can put the ingredients in a large zipper-top plastic bag and roll it with a rolling pin. Pour into a small bowl.

3. Place the beaten eggs in a shallow bowl. Dip the chicken pieces into the eggs and then dredge them in the corn chip mixture.

4. Bake until crispy and cooked through, 30 to 35 minutes.

5. Serve with the ranch dressing for dipping.

Serves 4 / **Per Serving**   Calories: 439   Protein: 39 grams
Sugar: 1 gram   Fat: 14 grams

Slow-Cooker Turkey Porcupine Meatballs

NUT-FREE   SOY-FREE

Prep time: 20 minutes   **Cook time:** 15 minutes on the stove top plus 8 hours in the slow cooker

"Porcupine" meatballs contain rice as a filler instead of bread crumbs so that they can be enjoyed on a low-FODMAP diet. The rice gives the meatballs the look of porcupine quills. Make this recipe in the morning, and allow it to cook on low in a slow cooker all day for an easy evening meal. If you don't have a slow cooker, you can bake the meatballs in a 375°F oven in a covered baking pan for 1 hour.

$1\frac{1}{2}$ pounds ground turkey

1 large egg, beaten

$\frac{1}{2}$ cup lactose-free whole milk

$\frac{2}{3}$ cup uncooked white rice

1 teaspoon sea salt

$\frac{1}{4}$ teaspoon freshly ground black pepper

2 tablespoons Garlic Oil (page 220)

6 scallions (green part only), diced

1 (14. 5-ounce) can diced tomatoes, with their juice

1 (8-ounce) can tomato sauce

1 teaspoon dried basil

$\frac{1}{2}$ cup Vegetable Stock (page 99)

1. In a large bowl, combine the ground turkey, egg, milk, white rice, $\frac{1}{2}$ teaspoon of the sea salt, and the pepper. Mix with your hands until the ingredients are combined. Roll into $1\frac{1}{2}$-inch balls.

2. Heat the garlic oil in a large skillet over medium-high heat until it shimmers. Brown the meatballs on all sides, about 5 minutes. Remove them from the fat in the skillet and place them in the slow cooker. ➤

Slow-Cooker Turkey Porcupine Meatballs continued

3. Add the scallion greens to the skillet and cook until they soften, about 4 minutes. Stir in the tomatoes, tomato sauce, basil, vegetable stock, and remaining ½ teaspoon salt. Scrape up any browned bits from the bottom of the pan. Bring to a simmer.

4. Pour the sauce over the meatballs in the slow cooker. Cover and set the cooker to low. Cook for 8 to 9 hours. Serve.

Serves 6 / **Per Serving**   Calories: 386   Protein: 36 grams
Sugar: 5 grams   Fat: 19 grams

Pan-Seared Duck Breast with Spicy Orange Pan Sauce

NUT-FREE   PALEO-FRIENDLY   DAIRY-FREE   SOY-FREE

Prep time: 15 minutes   **Cook time:** 20 minutes

For best results, duck should be cooked to medium-rare. Leave the skin on while you cook, since the skin and fat beneath it imparts a great deal of flavor. To render the fat fully, score the skin in a crosshatch pattern, cutting only through the fat and not into the meat below.

4 boneless, skin-on duck breast halves

Sea salt

Freshly ground black pepper

2 tablespoons unsalted butter

3 scallions (green part only), finely minced

1 cup freshly squeezed orange juice

$\frac{1}{4}$ cup dry white wine

$\frac{1}{2}$ teaspoon cayenne pepper

1 tablespoon olive oil

Zest of 1 orange, grated

1. Preheat the oven to 425°F.

2. Score the skin on each duck breast (see recipe introduction), and season liberally on both sides with salt and pepper.

3. In an oven-safe skillet, melt the butter over medium-high heat until it bubbles. Add the scallion greens and cook until they are fragrant. Stir in the orange juice, wine, and cayenne, and cook until the sauce is syrupy, 5 to 6 minutes. Pour the sauce into a small bowl and cover to keep warm.

4. Add the oil to the pan and heat it until it shimmers and coats the pan.   ➤

Pan-Seared Duck Breast with Spicy Orange Pan Sauce continued

5. Place the duck breasts in the pan, skin-side down. Cook without moving until the skin is brown and crisp and the fat is rendered, about 5 minutes. Drain the excess fat and turn the duck skin-side up.

6. Transfer the pan to the oven. Roast until the duck reaches an internal temperature of 155°F, 5 to 7 minutes. Allow the duck to rest for 10 minutes.

7. Remove the skin and discard. Cut the duck breast into ¼-inch-thick slices. Top with the sauce, sprinkle with the orange zest, and serve.

....

Serves 4 / **Per Serving** Calories: 331 Protein: 36 grams
Sugar: 6 grams Fat: 16 grams

Steak Fajitas with Bell Peppers

NUT-FREE   DAIRY-FREE   SOY-FREE

Prep time: 10 minutes, plus at least 1 hour to marinate   **Cook time:** 15 minutes

For the most flavorful results, prepare the marinade the night before you make these fajitas and marinate the meat overnight in a zipper-top plastic bag. You can also marinate the beef for a shorter time, as little as 1 hour, although it won't be as flavorful. Serve with Fresh Salsa (page 128).

$\frac{1}{4}$ cup chopped fresh cilantro

3 scallions (green part only), minced

$\frac{1}{2}$ jalapeño pepper, seeded

$\frac{1}{2}$ teaspoon ground cumin

Juice of 1 lime

3 tablespoons Garlic Oil (page 220)

1 pound flank steak

8 (6-inch) corn tortillas

2 green bell peppers, seeded and sliced

2 yellow bell peppers, seeded and sliced

1. In a food processor, pulse the cilantro, scallion greens, jalapeño, cumin, lime juice, and 2 tablespoons of the garlic oil until minced and combined but not pureed. You can also finely mince the cilantro, scallion greens, and jalapeño with a knife if you don't have a food processor, and then whisk in the cumin, lime juice, and garlic oil.

2. Place the flank steak in a zipper-top plastic bag and add the marinade. Seal the bag and push the steak around to coat it evenly. Place in the refrigerator to marinate for at least 1 hour, or overnight.

3. Preheat the oven to 350°F. Wrap the corn tortillas in foil and warm them in the oven for 15 minutes.   ➤

Steak Fajitas with Bell Peppers continued

4. Meanwhile, in a large sauté pan, heat the remaining 1 tablespoon garlic oil over medium-high heat until it shimmers. Add the flank steak and cook until it is browned on the outside and medium-rare in the center, 3 to 4 minutes per side. Remove the steak from pan and set it aside, tented with foil.

5. Add the peppers to the pan, and cook, stirring occasionally, until softened and brown, 5 to 6 minutes.

6. Slice the meat against the grain into ¼-inch-thick slices. Serve wrapped in corn tortillas with the peppers.

....

Serves 4 / **Per Serving**   Calories: 453   Protein: 36 grams
Sugar: 6 grams   Fat: 21 grams

Filet Mignon with Red Wine Pan Sauce

NUT-FREE   PALEO FRIENDLY   SOY-FREE

Prep time: 5 minutes   **Cook time:** 15 minutes

Filet mignon is a great special-occasion meal, and it cooks very quickly. This version is served topped with a flavorful red wine pan sauce. Serve with steamed vegetables and mashed potatoes, or with a simple side salad.

4 (4- to 6-ounce) beef tenderloin steaks (about 1½ inches thick)

Sea salt

Freshly ground black pepper

3 tablespoons Garlic Oil (page 220)

3 scallions (green part only), finely minced

1 cup dry red wine

1 teaspoon chopped fresh thyme

3 tablespoons cold unsalted butter, cut into ½-inch pieces

1. Season the steaks liberally with salt and pepper.

2. In a large sauté pan, heat the garlic oil over medium-high heat until it shimmers. Add the steaks and cook on one side until they are browned and seared, 3 to 4 minutes. Flip the steaks and cook on the other side until the meat reaches an internal temperature of 140°F to 145°F, 3 to 4 minutes. Remove the meat from the pan with tongs and set aside on a platter.

3. Add the scallion greens to the oil in the pan, and cook, stirring occasionally, until soft, 3 to 4 minutes. Add the red wine, scraping up the browned bits from the bottom of the pan. Stir in the thyme. Simmer, allowing the liquid to reduce to about ¼ cup. ➤

Filet Mignon with Red Wine Pan Sauce continued

4. Whisk in the butter, one piece at a time, until it is all incorporated.

5. Return the steaks to pan and turn once to coat with sauce. Serve with the sauce spooned over the top.

....

Serves 4 / **Per Serving**   Calories: 255   Protein: 32 grams
Sugar: 1 gram   Fat: 26 gram

INGREDIENT TIP

Never use cooking wine, which contains added salt. Instead, cook with wine that you would drink. Many flavorful wines are quite affordable, including boxed wines. Choose a dry red wine such as a Cabernet Sauvignon or Syrah for this recipe.

Easy Beefaroni

NUT-FREE   SOY-FREE

Prep time: 10 minutes   **Cook time:** 25 minutes

This kid-friendly recipe is a great way to stretch your meal budget, and it can be on your table in about 35 minutes. To keep fat to a minimum, use extra-lean ground beef. You can also use ground turkey or chicken in this recipe.

1 pound gluten-free elbow macaroni

2 tablespoons Garlic Oil (page 220)

1 pound lean ground beef

2 (15-ounce) cans crushed tomatoes

Sea salt

Freshly ground black pepper

2 cups shredded cheddar cheese

1. Preheat the oven to 350°F.

2. Bring a large pot of water to a boil over high heat. Add the elbow macaroni and cook according to the package instructions until al dente, 7 to 11 minutes.

3. Meanwhile, in a large skillet, heat the oil over medium-high heat until it shimmers. Add the ground beef and cook, breaking up the meat with a wooden spoon as it cooks, until browned, about 5 minutes.

4. Add the tomatoes, scraping up any browned bits from the bottom of the pan. Season with salt and pepper. Bring to a simmer.

5. Drain the pasta and pour it into a large casserole dish. Add the ground beef mixture and cheese and stir to combine well.

6. Bake until hot and bubbly, 20 to 25 minutes. Serve.

Serves 8 / Per Serving   Calories: 502   Protein: 34 grams
Sugar: 8 grams   Fat: 17 grams

Meatloaf "Muffins"

NUT-FREE   SOY-FREE

Prep time: 10 minutes   **Cook time:** 25 minutes

Meatloaf takes over an hour to cook, but these meatloaf "muffins" save you time and effort. Serve them with mashed potatoes or steamed vegetables, and top with Low-FODMAP Ketchup (page 227) or Low-FODMAP Barbecue Sauce (page 228).

2 tablespoons Garlic Oil (page 220)

6 scallions (green part only), finely minced

1 green bell pepper, seeded and chopped

$1\frac{1}{2}$ pounds ground beef

1 cup gluten-free bread crumbs

1 large egg, beaten

$\frac{1}{2}$ cup lactose-free whole milk

1 tablespoon Dijon mustard

1 tablespoon prepared horseradish

1 tablespoon gluten-free soy sauce

1 teaspoon dried thyme

$\frac{1}{2}$ teaspoon sea salt

$\frac{1}{2}$ teaspoon freshly ground black pepper

$\frac{1}{4}$ teaspoon cayenne pepper

1. Preheat the oven to 450°F. Coat a 12-cup muffin tin with nonstick cooking spray and set aside.

2. In a medium sauté pan, heat the garlic oil over medium-high heat until it shimmers. Add the scallion greens and green peppers, and cook until soft, 3 to 4 minutes. Remove from the heat and set aside to cool.

3. In a large bowl, combine the cooled scallion greens and peppers, ground beef, bread crumbs, egg, milk, Dijon, horseradish, soy sauce, thyme, salt, black pepper, and cayenne. Using your hands, mix it all together gently until well combined.

4. Spoon the meatloaf mixture evenly among the 12 muffin cups. Bake until the internal temperature of each meatloaf "muffin" reaches 165°F, about 20 minutes. Serve.

....

Serves 6 / **Per Serving** Calories: 358   Protein: 39 grams
Sugar: 3 grams   Fat: 14 grams

Thin-Cut Pork Chops with Mustard-Chive Pan Sauce

NUT-FREE   PALEO-FRIENDLY   DAIRY-FREE   SOY-FREE

Prep time: 5 minutes   **Cook time:** 30 minutes

Using thin-cut pork chops allows you to pan-sear them over high heat very quickly, so they don't have time to dry out. The savory mustard sauce perfectly complements the flavor of pork. Choose a dry white wine such as Chardonnay for the sauce.

8 (2-ounce) boneless thin-cut pork loin chops

Sea salt

Freshly ground black pepper

2 tablespoons Garlic Oil (page 220)

3 scallions (green part only), finely minced

1 cup dry white wine

2 tablespoons Dijon mustard

2 tablespoons chopped fresh chives

1. Season the pork chops liberally with salt and pepper.

2. Heat the oil in a large nonstick skillet over medium-high heat until it shimmers. Working in batches so you don't crowd the pan, cook the pork until it browns, about 3 minutes per side. Set the pork aside on a platter, tented with foil to keep warm.

3. Add the scallion greens to the pan and cook until they soften, stirring occasionally, about 3 minutes. Add the wine to the pan, scraping up any browned bits from the bottom of the pan. Whisk in the mustard. Bring to a simmer and cook until about $1/2$ cup remains, about 20 minutes. Stir in the chives.

4. Return the pork to the pan. Turn it to coat with the sauce and cook for 1 more minute to reheat. Serve with the mustard sauce spooned over the pork.

Serves 4 / **Per Serving**   Calories: 481   Protein: 26 grams
Sugar: 1 gram   Fat: 35 grams

Slow-Cooker Pulled Pork Sandwiches with Ginger Slaw

NUT-FREE   DAIRY-FREE   SOY-FREE

Prep time: 15 minutes   **Cook time:** 9 hours in the slow cooker

This is the perfect meal for a busy weeknight. Prepare the pork in the morning before you go to work, and then cook it on low in a slow cooker all day. Then when you're ready for dinner, whip up the slaw and serve with a side salad or raw veggies. If you don't have a slow cooker, you can cut the pork shoulder into 4-ounce chunks, rub it with the spice mixture, and brown it on all sides in a Dutch oven over medium-high heat. Then add the remaining ingredients, lower the heat, and simmer until the pork is fork-tender, about 1 hour.

FOR THE PULLED PORK

3 tablespoons dark brown sugar

2 teaspoons smoked paprika

$\frac{1}{2}$ teaspoon ground cumin

$\frac{1}{2}$ teaspoon sea salt

$\frac{1}{2}$ teaspoon freshly ground black pepper

1 (3 pound) boneless pork shoulder, trimmed

1 cup Low-FODMAP Barbecue Sauce (page 228)

FOR THE SLAW

1 head green cabbage, cored and shredded

1 large carrot, peeled and grated

3 scallions (green part only), thinly sliced

3 tablespoons white vinegar

2 teaspoons Garlic Oil (page 220)

$1\frac{1}{2}$ teaspoons peeled grated ginger

Dash red pepper flakes

FOR THE ASSEMBLY

6 gluten-free hamburger buns   ➤

Slow-Cooker Pulled Pork Sandwiches with Ginger Slaw continued

TO MAKE THE PULLED PORK

1. In a small bowl, combine the brown sugar, paprika, cumin, salt, and pepper. Rub all over the pork roast.

2. Place the pork in the slow cooker. Add the barbecue sauce. Cover and cook on low until the pork is fork-tender, 9 to 10 hours.

3. Remove the pork from sauce. Pull the meat apart with two forks.

4. Skim the fat from sauce. Pour the sauce into a small saucepan and simmer until it thickens, about 10 minutes.

TO MAKE THE SLAW

1. Combine the cabbage, carrot, and scallion greens in a large bowl.

2. In a small bowl, whisk together the vinegar, oil, ginger, and pepper flakes. Toss with the cabbage mixture to coat.

TO ASSEMBLE THE SANDWICHES

1. Toast the hamburger buns.

2. Mix the sauce with the shredded pork. Spoon the pork onto the toasted buns. Top with the slaw and serve.

Serves 6 / **Per Serving**   Calories: 576   Protein: 65 grams
Sugar: 22 grams   Fat: 12 grams

INGREDIENT TIP

Pork shoulder is at its most tender when you cook it low and slow. Cooking longer than the 9 hours won't hurt the pork. Once it is fully cooked and shredded, you can also mix it with the barbecue sauce and hold it in the slow cooker on the "keep warm" setting for several hours, if you wish.

Make sure the amount of green cabbage used in this recipe does not exceed six cups; more than that, and you will exceed the FODMAP load for this meal.

Minted Lamb Chops

NUT-FREE   PALEO-FRIENDLY   DAIRY-FREE   SOY-FREE

Prep time: 15 minutes   **Cook time:** 10 minutes

Fresh mint cuts beautifully through the gaminess sometimes associated with lamb. This recipe is an updated low-FODMAP take on the classic lamb with mint sauce. Instead of a sweet sauce, the lamb chops are cooked with fresh mint that lends its flavor without being cloying or overwhelming.

4 (4- to 5-ounce) lamb loin chops

¼ cup Garlic Oil (page 220)

¼ cup chopped fresh mint

2 teaspoons ground cumin

1 teaspoon ground coriander

1 teaspoon sea salt

1 teaspoon freshly ground black pepper

Dash cayenne pepper

1. Preheat the broiler. Place the lamb chops on a broiler pan.

2. In a food processor, pulse the garlic oil, mint, cumin, coriander, salt, black pepper, and cayenne briefly until just combined but not pureed.

3. Spread the mixture on top of the lamb chops, and allow them to sit at room temperature for 15 minutes.

4. Broil the lamb chops, turning once, until they are browned on both sides and the meat reaches an internal temperature of 145°F, about 10 minutes. Serve.

Serves 4 / **Per Serving**   Calories: 334   Protein: 32 grams
Sugar: 0 grams   Fat: 22 grams

Easy Lamb Stew

NUT-FREE   DAIRY-FREE   SOY-FREE

Prep time: 15 minutes   **Cook time:** 30 minutes

This lamb stew is full of healthy goodness. Along with ground lamb, the stew contains healthy vegetables including red bell peppers, carrots, kale, and tomatoes. If you don't care for lamb, you can replace it with an equal amount of ground beef, turkey, or chicken.

  2 tablespoons Garlic Oil (page 220)
  1 pound ground lamb
  1 leek (green part only), diced
  1 celery stalk, chopped
  1 carrot, peeled and chopped
  1 red bell pepper, seeded and chopped
  2 tablespoons gluten-free all-purpose flour
  2 cups Vegetable Stock (page 99)
  1 bunch kale, stems removed and leaves chopped
  1 (14. 5-ounce) can crushed tomatoes
  2 teaspoons chopped fresh thyme
  Sea salt
  Freshly ground black pepper

1. In a large sauté pan over medium-high, heat the garlic oil until it shimmers. Add the lamb and cook, breaking up the meat with a wooden spoon, until it browns, about 5 minutes. Remove the lamb from the oil with a slotted spoon and set aside to drain on paper towels.

2. In the oil that remains in the pan, cook the leek, celery, carrot, and bell pepper until the vegetables soften and begin to brown, about 5 minutes.

3. Add the flour and cook, stirring constantly, until it turns golden, about 3 minutes.

4. Stir in the vegetable stock, scraping up any browned bits from the bottom of the pan. Stir in the kale, crushed tomatoes, thyme, and lamb. Bring to a simmer and cook, stirring occasionally, until the kale is tender, about 15 more minutes. Season with salt and pepper and serve.

....

Serves 4 / **Per Serving** Calories: 383   Protein: 38 grams
Sugar: 10 grams   Fat: 16 grams

10

Desserts

Lemon-Rosemary Granita

NUT-FREE   VEGETARIAN   VEGAN   DAIRY-FREE   SOY-FREE

Prep time: 10 minutes, plus freezing and stirring time   **Cook time:** 10 minutes

This granita is a sweet treat with just a hint of savory. If you can, select Meyer lemons since they are juicier and slightly sweeter than regular lemons and have a more pronounced lemon flavor. The rosemary complements the lemon perfectly— be sure to use fresh rosemary, not dried. The granita will need several cycles of freezing and stirring to give it the right texture, but most of the time spent is just waiting for it to freeze.

  3 cups water
  1 cup plus 2 tablespoons sugar
  5 rosemary sprigs
  Zest of 1 lemon
  Juice of 6 lemons

1. In a medium saucepan over medium-high heat, bring the water, sugar, rosemary, and lemon zest to a simmer. Simmer, stirring constantly, until the sugar dissolves. Remove from the heat, cover, and allow the mixture to steep for 10 minutes.

2. Strain the syrup through a fine-mesh sieve into a large bowl and stir in the lemon juice. Whisk to combine.

3. Cover and chill in the refrigerator until cold, about 15 minutes.

4. Pour the chilled mixture into two 9-by-9-inch shallow baking pans and freeze. After 15 minutes, stir the granita with a large fork. Continue stirring and freezing in 15-minute increments until completely frozen, about 1 hour. Serve.

Serves 4 / **Per Serving**   Calories: 232   Protein: 1 gram
Sugar: 58 grams   Fat: 1 gram

Honeydew-Mint Sorbet

Prep time: 15 minutes, plus freezing time   **Cook time:** 5 minutes

Sorbet is a smooth frozen fruit dessert made from pureed fruit and simple syrup. The great trick about this recipe is you can make endless variations, depending on the fruit and flavorings you choose. For example, you can infuse the syrup with thyme, rosemary, or tarragon. You can replace the honeydew with cantaloupe, or use low-FODMAP fruits like berries.

$3/4$ cup packed chopped fresh mint, plus 2 tablespoons chopped fresh mint

$1/2$ cup sugar

$1/2$ cup water

3 cups honeydew melon, peeled, seeded, and cubed

1 tablespoon freshly squeezed lemon juice

1. In a small saucepan over medium-high heat, bring $3/4$ cup of the mint, the sugar, and the water to a simmer. Simmer for 5 minutes. Remove from the heat, cover, and allow the mixture to steep for 10 minutes.

2. Strain the syrup through a fine-mesh sieve into a blender jar. Add the honeydew melon, the remaining 2 tablespoons mint, and the lemon juice. Blend on high until pureed.

3. Pour the mixture into a 9-by-13-inch baking pan and freeze until firm, 2 to 3 hours. Puree the sorbet in the blender before serving.

Serves 4 / **Per Serving**   Calories: 193   Protein: 1 gram
Sugar: 45 grams   Fat: 0.5 gram

Lime Curd with Meringue Topping

NUT-FREE   VEGETARIAN   SOY-FREE

Prep time: 20 minutes   **Cook time:** 6 minutes

This recipe is like lime meringue pie without the crust. Use fresh lime juice to make the curd, because commercially prepared juice may impart off flavors. Because meringue contains raw eggs, it is best to choose eggs that are less than a week old, or use pasteurized eggs.

FOR THE LIME CURD

3 large eggs

$\frac{1}{2}$ cup sugar

$\frac{1}{2}$ cup freshly squeezed lime juice

2 teaspoons finely grated fresh lime zest

6 tablespoons unsalted butter, cut into pieces

FOR THE MERINGUE

4 large egg whites

Pinch cream of tartar

2 tablespoons sugar

TO MAKE THE LIME CURD

1. In a large saucepan, whisk the eggs, sugar, lime juice, and lime zest. Place the pan over low heat, and add the butter, one piece at a time, whisking constantly. Cook until the curd begins to bubble and thicken, about 6 minutes.

2. Transfer to a bowl, cover, and chill while you make the meringue.

Place the egg whites and cream of tartar in a bowl, and use a hand mixer or stand mixer with a whisk attachment to beat the eggs to soft peaks. Continue beating as you add the sugar gradually, until stiff peaks form.

TO ASSEMBLE

1. Divide the lime curd among four dessert cups. Top with the meringue.

2. If you wish, you may brown the top of the meringue with a kitchen torch.

Serves 4 / **Per Serving**   Calories: 346   Protein: 9 grams
Sugar: 32 grams   Fat: 21 grams

TIME-SAVING TIP

For best results and to save time with the meringue, make sure there isn't even a speck of yolks in the egg whites, and whip them at room temperature. Cold egg whites take much longer to whip, and even a tiny amount of yolk in the whites hampers the process.

Maple-Glazed Grilled Pineapple

Prep time: 5 minutes   **Cook time:** 6 minutes

Grilling fruit caramelizes the sugars in the fruit, so it is sweeter and more delicious. To add flavor, the pineapple in this recipe is brushed with pure maple syrup, which also caramelizes and adds complexity to the dish. If you don't have a grill, you can bake the pineapple slices on a rimmed baking sheet in a 350°F oven for 10 minutes.

1 pineapple, peeled, cored, and cut into 1-inch-thick rings

¼ cup pure maple syrup

1. Heat the grill to high. Lightly oil the grate.

2. Brush the pineapple on both sides with the maple syrup, and place on the grill. Grill until heated through, about 3 minutes per side. Serve.

Serves 8 / **Per Serving**   Calories: 26   Protein: 0 grams
Sugar: 6 grams   Fat: 0 grams

Strawberry Shortcake

NUT-FREE   VEGETARIAN   SOY-FREE

Prep time: 10 minutes   **Cook time:** 10 minutes

To make this shortcake, you must first make your own gluten-free baking mix and then measure that baking mix into the recipe. The baking mix (recipe follows) will keep tightly sealed for 3 months for use in other recipes, such as Low-FODMAP Pancakes (page 70).

FOR THE GLUTEN-FREE BAKING MIX

$1\frac{1}{2}$ cups rice flour

$1\frac{1}{2}$ cups potato starch

3 tablespoons sugar

$1\frac{1}{2}$ tablespoons baking powder

1 teaspoon salt

FOR THE SHORTCAKE

4 cups sliced strawberries

$\frac{1}{2}$ cup sugar

$2\frac{1}{3}$ cups gluten-free baking mix

$\frac{1}{3}$ cup unsalted butter, cut into pieces

3 large eggs, beaten

$\frac{3}{4}$ cup lactose-free whole milk

$\frac{1}{2}$ teaspoon pure vanilla extract

TO MAKE THE BAKING MIX

In a medium-sized bowl, whisk the rice flour, potato starch, sugar, baking powder, and salt until well combined.

TO MAKE THE SHORTCAKE

1. Preheat the oven to 425°F. Grease a baking sheet and set aside.

2. In a small bowl, combine the strawberries and $\frac{1}{4}$ cup of the sugar. Set aside. ➤

Strawberry Shortcake continued

3. In a medium-sized bowl, combine the baking mix and the remaining ¼ cup of sugar. Cut in the butter using two knives or a pastry blender until the mixture resembles coarse sand.

4. In another bowl, whisk together the eggs, milk, and vanilla. Pour the wet mixture into the baking mixture and stir until just combined.

5. Divide the dough into 6 pieces, and drop them onto the prepared baking sheet. Bake until the biscuits brown, about 10 minutes. Allow them to cool for 10 minutes.

6. Carefully split the biscuits. Spoon the strawberry mixture over the top and serve.

....

Serves 6 / **Per Serving**   Calories: 408   Protein: 9 grams
Sugar: 23 grams   Fat: 14 grams

TIME-SAVING TIP

To save time, you can replace the homemade gluten-free baking mix with an equal amount of Bisquick Gluten-Free Baking Mix. You can also replace the fresh strawberries with thawed frozen strawberries as long as they don't contain high-fructose corn syrup (HFCS) as an additive.

Oat Crumble with Rhubarb Sauce

VEGETARIAN   SOY-FREE

Prep time: 10 minutes, plus chilling time   **Cook time:** 35 minutes

Rhubarb sauce is sweet and sour at the same time. Many people are surprised to learn that rhubarb is actually a vegetable because it is most often used as a fruit in recipes. Cut the rhubarb into $\frac{1}{2}$-inch pieces.

FOR THE RHUBARB SAUCE
$\frac{1}{2}$ cup granulated sugar

$\frac{1}{2}$ cup water

4 cups chopped rhubarb

$\frac{1}{2}$ teaspoon ground cinnamon

FOR THE OAT CRUMBLE
$\frac{1}{2}$ cup gluten-free all-purpose flour

$\frac{1}{2}$ cup gluten-free oats

$\frac{1}{2}$ cup brown sugar

$\frac{1}{4}$ cup chopped walnuts

1 teaspoon ground cinnamon

$\frac{1}{3}$ cup cold unsalted butter, cut into $\frac{1}{2}$-inch cubes

TO MAKE THE RHUBARB SAUCE

1. In a medium-sized saucepan over medium-high heat, bring the granulated sugar, water, and rhubarb to a boil. Reduce the heat and simmer, stirring occasionally, until the rhubarb is tender, about 10 minutes.

2. Remove from the heat and stir in the cinnamon. Chill completely.   ➤

Oat Crumble with Rhubarb Sauce continued

TO MAKE THE OAT CRUMBLE

1. Preheat the oven to 375°F. Line a baking sheet with parchment paper and set aside.

2. Combine the flour, oats, brown sugar, walnuts, cinnamon, and butter in a bowl. Using your fingers, mix by pinching the ingredients together until it combines into a crumble.

3. Scatter the crumble on the prepared baking sheet. Bake until brown, 20 to 25 minutes.

4. Pour the chilled rhubarb sauce into a serving bowl. Sprinkle the crumble over the rhubarb sauce and serve.

Serves 4 / **Per Serving**   Calories: 521   Protein: 4 grams
Sugar: 44 grams   Fat: 28 grams

Mixed Berry Yogurt Ice Pops

NUT-FREE   VEGETARIAN   SOY-FREE

Prep time: 5 minutes, plus 5 hours freezing time   **Cook time:** None

Nothing is more refreshing on a summer day than an ice pop. These ice pops get their creaminess from plain lactose-free yogurt. If you don't have ice pop molds, you can freeze the ice pops in paper cups. Simply cover the top of each cup with foil and poke an ice pop stick through the foil to hold it in place. Remove the foil and peel away the cup when you're ready to eat.

2 cups plain lactose-free yogurt

1 cup fresh blueberries

$\frac{1}{2}$ cup fresh strawberries

$\frac{1}{2}$ cup fresh raspberries

$\frac{1}{4}$ cup sugar

1. Combine the yogurt, berries, and sugar in a blender, and blend until the fruit is pureed. Pour into eight ice pop molds.

2. Freeze until the ice pops are solid, about 5 hours. Serve.

Serves 8 / **Per Serving**   Calories: 84   Protein: 4 grams
Sugar: 13 grams   Fat: 1 gram

Lemon Squares

Prep time: 10 minutes   **Cook time:** 50 minutes

Lemon bars are an American favorite, featuring lemon curd on a shortbread crust. This version uses gluten-free baking mix. If you'd like to save time, you can replace the homemade baking mix with Bisquick Gluten-Free Baking Mix. Don't sprinkle the bars with powdered sugar until you are ready to serve them, or the sugar will melt into the lemon curd.

2 cups Gluten-Free Baking Mix (page 201)
$\frac{1}{2}$ cup powdered sugar, plus more for sprinkling
1 cup unsalted butter, at room temperature
4 large eggs
$1\frac{1}{3}$ cups granulated sugar
3 tablespoons gluten-free all-purpose flour
$\frac{1}{3}$ cup lactose-free whole milk
Juice of 4 large lemons
2 teaspoons grated fresh lemon zest
$\frac{1}{8}$ teaspoon salt
Powdered sugar, for sprinkling

1. Preheat the oven to 350°F.

2. In a large bowl, mix the gluten-free baking mix, powdered sugar, and butter into a crumbly but well blended mixture. Press it into the bottom of a 9-by-13-inch baking pan. Bake until the crust is lightly browned, about 20 minutes.

3. While the crust bakes, in a medium-sized bowl, whisk together the eggs, granulated sugar, and gluten-free flour. Whisk in the milk, lemon juice, lemon zest, and salt.

4. Reduce the oven temperature to 325°F. Pour the lemon filling over the warm crust. Bake until the filling is firm, about 20 minutes. Cool completely.

5. Cut into squares and sprinkle with the powdered sugar just before serving.

....

Makes 24 squares / **Per Serving (1 square)**   Calories: 196   Protein: 3 grams
Sugar: 14 grams   Fat: 9 grams

Orange-Vanilla Smoothie

NUT-FREE   VEGETARIAN   SOY-FREE

Prep time: 5 minutes, plus 20 minutes resting time   **Cook time:** None

This delicious dessert smoothie tastes just like an orange Creamsicle.
If you'd like a more intense orange flavor, add 1 teaspoon freshly grated
orange zest. Use freshly squeezed orange juice for this recipe.

   1 cup freshly squeezed orange juice
   ¼ cup chia seeds
   2 cups lactose-free plain yogurt
   1 cup lactose-free whole milk
   ¼ cup sugar
   2 teaspoons pure vanilla extract
   1 cup crushed ice

1. In a small bowl, combine the orange juice and chia seeds. Allow the mixture to sit for 20 minutes in order for the chia seeds to thicken and expand.

2. In a blender, combine the orange juice–chia mixture, yogurt, milk, sugar, vanilla, and crushed ice. Blend on high until smooth. Serve.

Serves 4 / **Per Serving**   Calories: 355   Protein: 16 grams
Sugar: 30 grams   Fat: 13 grams

Berry Summer Pudding

NUT-FREE   VEGETARIAN   VEGAN   DAIRY-FREE   SOY-FREE

Prep time: 10 minutes, plus overnight refrigeration   **Cook time:** 10 minutes

Summer pudding is a British treat that is quite different from pudding typically found in the United States. Instead of being a dairy-based product, summer pudding is made from berries and day-old bread. Use stale bread, because it allows the juice from the berries to soak in much more easily.

1 cup sugar
3 tablespoons water
2 cups raspberries
1 cup golden raspberries
2 cups sliced strawberries
1 cup blueberries
8 slices day-old gluten-free sandwich bread

1. Line a large bowl with plastic wrap.

2. In a large saucepan over medium high-heat, bring the sugar, water, and berries to a simmer. Simmer for 5 minutes to release the juices. Allow the berries to cool slightly.

3. Remove the crusts from the bread. Cut the bread in half on the diagonal. Using eight triangles of bread (or more if needed), dip each piece in the berries, and then line the bowl with the bread, trimming as necessary.

4. Using a slotted spoon, spoon the fruit (reserving the liquid) over the bread in the bowl.

5. Dip the remaining eight triangles of bread in the liquid and place them over the berries. Pour any of the remaining juices over the top of the pudding. ➤

Berry Summer Pudding continued

6. Cover with plastic wrap. Place a small plate (one that will fit over the pudding but inside of the bowl) over the top and weight it with a few heavy cans. Refrigerate overnight.

7. When ready to serve, remove the weights, plate, and plastic wrap. Place a large plate over the bowl and invert to unmold the pudding. Remove the plastic wrap. Cut into slices and serve.

....

Serves 12 / **Per Serving**   Calories: 171   Protein: 1.9 grams
Sugar: 20 grams   Fat: 3 grams

Butterscotch Pudding

NUT-FREE   VEGETARIAN   SOY-FREE

Prep time: 5 minutes, plus time for refrigeration   **Cook time:** 10 minutes

Homemade butterscotch pudding is so much tastier than instant pudding, which uses artificial flavorings. Butterscotch is a simple combination of butter and brown sugar. Use dark brown sugar, unsalted butter, and lactose-free whole milk for best flavor.

3 tablespoons unsalted butter

3 tablespoons dark brown sugar

2½ cups lactose-free whole milk

3 tablespoons cornstarch

3 tablespoons water

1 teaspoon pure vanilla extract

Pinch salt

1. In a medium saucepan over medium-high heat, melt the butter. Stir in the brown sugar and bring the mixture to a boil. Stir in ½ cup of the milk and simmer, stirring constantly, until the sugar dissolves completely. Remove the pan from the heat and stir in the remaining 2 cups milk.

2. Combine the cornstarch and water in a small dish, stirring until smooth.

3. Return the pudding to medium heat and slowly add the cornstarch slurry, stirring constantly. Continue stirring until the pudding begins to thicken and comes to a slow simmer. Once the pudding simmers, cook it for 1 minute, stirring constantly. Remove the pudding from heat, and stir in the vanilla and salt.

4. Pour the pudding into four custard cups and chill until set, 2 to 4 hours. Serve.

Serves 4 / Per Serving   Calories: 222   Protein: 5 grams
Sugar: 14 grams   Fat: 14 grams

Crêpes with Blueberry Filling

NUT-FREE   VEGETARIAN   SOY-FREE

Prep time: 5 minutes   **Cook time:** 15 minutes

Crêpes are traditional thin French pancakes. Here the crêpes are used in a sweet dish, but you can also enjoy crêpes with savory fillings such as seafood or meat. Traditional crêpes contain dairy and wheat flour, but this recipe is both dairy-free and gluten-free. For a richer crêpe, you can replace the rice milk with lactose-free whole milk and the oil with melted unsalted butter.

$1^1/_4$ cups unsweetened rice milk

2 large eggs

2 tablespoons canola oil, plus more for the skillet

1 cup gluten-free all-purpose flour

$^1/_4$ cup plus 1 teaspoon granulated sugar

$^1/_8$ teaspoon baking powder

Pinch salt

1 pint blueberries

Juice of 1 lemon

Powdered sugar, for garnish

1. Preheat the oven to 200°F. Line an oven-safe platter with parchment.

2. In a blender, combine the rice milk, eggs, and oil. Blend until well mixed.

3. In a small bowl, whisk together the flour, 1 teaspoon of the granulated sugar, the baking powder, and the salt. Add the mixture to the blender and blend until smooth.

4. Heat an 8-inch nonstick skillet over medium heat. Brush a small amount of oil in the bottom of the skillet. Pour $^1/_4$ cup of the crêpe batter into the skillet, swirling the pan to coat it with batter. Cook for 1 minute. Gently flip the crêpe and cook for 1 minute more. Place the crêpe on the prepared platter, and top it with another piece of parchment. Repeat this step for the remaining crêpes. Place the crêpes in the oven to keep warm.

5. In a medium-sized saucepan over medium-high heat, cook the blueberries, the remaining ¼ cup granulated sugar, and the lemon juice until the blueberries release their juice and the sugar is dissolved, about 5 minutes.

6. Spoon some of the warm filling in each crêpe, roll it up, and garnish with powdered sugar. Serve.

....

Serves 6 / **Per Serving**   Calories: 238   Protein: 5 grams
Sugar: 16 grams   Fat: 7 grams

TIME-SAVING TIP

You can make both the crêpes and the blueberry filling ahead of time if you wish, so they're ready to serve quickly. To save the crêpes for later, cover the final crêpe with parchment and wrap all of the crêpes and parchment in plastic or place it in a large zipper-top plastic bag. To save the blueberries, seal tightly and refrigerate. Both will keep for up to 3 days in the refrigerator.

Orange-Almond Dutch Baby

VEGETARIAN   SOY-FREE

Prep time: 10 minutes   **Cook time:** 25 minutes

A Dutch baby is a puffed pancake. In this recipe, it is glazed with a sweet orange syrup, making for a light, custardy, and delicious dessert. You can also serve it as an easy breakfast, topped with pure maple syrup.

2 tablespoons unsalted butter

3 large eggs

$\frac{1}{2}$ cup lactose-free whole milk

$\frac{1}{2}$ teaspoon pure almond extract

$\frac{1}{2}$ cup gluten-free all-purpose flour

Pinch salt

$\frac{1}{4}$ cup powdered sugar

Juice of 3 oranges

1. Preheat the oven to 375°F. Place the butter in a 9-inch deep-dish pie plate and put it in the oven, allowing the butter to melt.

2. Put the eggs, milk, and almond extract in a blender and blend to combine.

3. In a small bowl, whisk together the flour and salt. Add to the blender and blend until all the ingredients are combined and the batter is smooth.

4. Remove the pan from the oven, swirling to distribute the melted butter. Carefully pour the batter into the butter. Bake until the Dutch baby browns slightly and puffs, about 25 minutes.

5. Remove the Dutch baby from the oven. Cut it into four wedges. The Dutch baby will collapse as you cut it; this is normal.

6. Sprinkle the powdered sugar over the top of each wedge, and then squeeze the orange juice over the top of the powdered sugar. Serve warm.

Serves 4 / **Per Serving**   Calories: 271   Protein: 9 grams
Sugar: 22 grams   Fat: 10 grams

Peanut Butter Cookies

VEGETARIAN   DAIRY-FREE   SOY-FREE

Prep time: 5 minutes   **Cook time:** 8 minutes

These simple cookies contain only four ingredients. Even though they don't contain leavening agents or flour, they definitely taste like cookies. While this recipe calls for finely chopped peanuts, you can replace them with vegan mini chocolate chips, if you wish. The cookies will keep in a tightly sealed container at room temperature for 1 week.

1 cup peanut butter
1 cup light brown sugar
1 large egg, beaten
2 tablespoons chopped peanuts

1. Preheat the oven to 350°F. Line a baking sheet with parchment and set aside.

2. In a small bowl, combine the peanut butter, brown sugar, and egg until well mixed. Gently stir in the chopped peanuts.

3. Drop by the spoonful onto the prepared baking sheet, leaving room for the cookies to spread.

4. Bake until the cookies are just browned on the bottoms, 6 to 8 minutes.

5. Allow the cookies to rest on the cookie sheet for 10 minutes, and then transfer them with a spatula to a parchment-lined wire rack to cool. Serve.

Makes 12 cookies / Per Serving (1 cookie)   Calories: 186   Protein: 6 grams
Sugar: 14 grams   Fat: 12 grams

Lemon Meringue Shells with Raspberries

NUT-FREE   VEGETARIAN   DAIRY-FREE   SOY-FREE

Prep time: 10 minutes   **Cook time:** 1 hour, plus resting time

Tart raspberries cradled in light, lemony meringue shells are perfect desserts for warm summer nights. Because fresh raspberries are highly perishable, wait until you need to use the berries before washing them. Washing will make them more prone to spoiling.

$3/4$ cup sugar

2 teaspoons finely grated fresh lemon zest

3 large egg whites, at room temperature

$1/4$ teaspoon cream of tartar

1 pint raspberries

1. Preheat the oven to 275°F. Line a baking sheet with parchment. Trace eight 3-inch circles on the parchment to use as a guide.

2. Put the sugar and lemon zest in a food processor, and pulse briefly until combined.

3. In a large mixing bowl (or in the bowl of a stand mixer), use an electric mixer with the whisk attachment to beat the egg whites until foamy. Add the cream of tartar and continue beating until the eggs form soft peaks. Continuing to beat on high speed, slowly add the lemon sugar. Continue beating until the meringue forms stiff peaks.

4. In each circle marked on the parchment, gently spread $1/3$ cup of the meringue to fill the circle. Carefully create an indentation with the back of a spoon, forming shells.

5. Bake the shells for 1 hour. Turn off the oven and allow the shells to sit for an additional $1^{1}/_{2}$ hours in the oven.

6. Transfer the baking sheet to a wire rack and allow it to rest for an additional 15 minutes, and then use a spatula to carefully transfer the meringues to the rack to cool completely.

7. Serve the cups filled with fresh raspberries.

....

Serves 8 / **Per Serving**   Calories: 97   Protein: 2 grams
Sugar: 20 grams   Fat: 0.3 gram

TIME-SAVING TIP

To save time, you can make the meringues up to a month ahead. Store them at room temperature in a tightly sealed container. The meringues will retain their crispiness as long as the seal is airtight.

11

Condiments, Sauces, and Dressings

Garlic Oil

NUT-FREE   VEGETARIAN   VEGAN   PALEO-FRIENDLY   DAIRY-FREE   SOY-FREE

Prep time: 5 minutes, plus resting time   **Cook time:** 10 minutes

Garlic oil is used in many recipes throughout this cookbook. While garlic contains FODMAPs, if you use it to flavor oil and then strain away all of the solids, it won't aggravate your IBS—but it will allow you to enjoy some garlic flavor.

1 cup extra-virgin olive oil
6 garlic cloves, sliced

1. Place the olive oil in a small saucepan over medium-low heat. Add the garlic and bring it to a simmer. Reduce the heat to low and simmer, stirring frequently, for 5 minutes.

2. Allow the oil to cool for at least 10 minutes, or longer for a stronger flavored oil. Strain the oil through a fine-mesh sieve and discard the solids.

3. Store in a tightly sealed container in the refrigerator for up to 1 week.

Makes 1 cup / **Per Serving (1 tablespoon)**   Calories: 120   Protein: 0 grams
Sugar: 0 grams   Fat: 14 grams

INGREDIENT VARIATION

You can also make Onion Oil, replacing the garlic with ½ sliced onion. For Garlic-Onion Oil, use ¼ sliced onion and 3 sliced garlic cloves.

Garlic-Basil Vinaigrette

Prep time: 5 minutes   **Cook time:** None

This vinaigrette is good on Pasta Salad with Ham and Vegetables (page 97) as well as other salads made from greens. You can also use it as a marinade for fish, meat, poultry, or tofu. Whisk the vinaigrette thoroughly before serving, or place it in a shaker bottle and shake it well.

$3/4$ cup Garlic Oil (page 220)

$1/4$ cup red wine vinegar

2 tablespoons finely chopped fresh basil

$1/4$ teaspoon sea salt

$1/8$ teaspoons freshly ground black pepper

Whisk together the oil, vinegar, basil, salt, and pepper in a small bowl. Serve immediately, or store in a tightly sealed container in the refrigerator for up to 1 week.

Makes 1 cup / **Per Serving (2 tablespoons)**   Calories: 182   Protein: 0 grams
Sugar: 0 grams   Fat: 20 grams

INGREDIENT VARIATION

For a traditional Italian dressing, add 1 teaspoon finely chopped fresh oregano and 1 tablespoon grated Parmesan cheese.

Balsamic Dijon Dressing

Prep time: 5 minutes   **Cook time:** None

Balsamic vinegar is low in FODMAPs, provided you limit yourself to 1 tablespoon. This salad dressing recipe uses a 3:1 vinaigrette ratio, so 2 tablespoons of dressing has less than 1 tablespoon of balsamic vinegar. Limit yourself to one 2-tablespoon serving per meal.

2 tablespoons balsamic vinegar

2 tablespoons Dijon mustard

$\frac{1}{4}$ teaspoon sea salt

$\frac{1}{8}$ teaspoon freshly ground black pepper

$\frac{3}{4}$ cup Garlic Oil (page 220)

1. In a small bowl, whisk together the vinegar, mustard, salt, and pepper until well combined. Add the oil in a thin stream, whisking to emulsify.

2. Serve immediately, or store in a tightly sealed container in the refrigerator for up to 1 week.

Makes 1 cup / **Per Serving (2 tablespoons)**   Calories: 184   Protein: 0 grams
Sugar: 0 grams   Fat: 20.6 grams

Orange–Poppy Seed Dressing

Prep time: 5 minutes   **Cook time:** None

Enjoy this delicious salad dressing on a spinach salad or on other mixed greens. It is also a tasty marinade for seafood, particularly salmon and shrimp.

2 tablespoons champagne vinegar

2 tablespoons freshly squeezed orange juice

1 teaspoon Dijon mustard

1 tablespoon finely minced fresh chives

3/4 cup Garlic Oil (page 220)

1 tablespoon poppy seeds

1. In a small bowl, whisk together the vinegar, orange juice, mustard, and chives. Add the garlic oil in a thin stream, whisking constantly to emulsify. Stir in the poppy seeds.

2. Serve immediately, or store in a tightly sealed container in the refrigerator for up to 1 week.

Makes 1 cup / Per Serving (2 tablespoons)   Calories: 184   Protein: 0 grams
Sugar: 0 grams   Fat: 20 grams

Low-FODMAP Mayonnaise

Prep time: 10 minutes   **Cook time:** None

Many brands of commercially prepared mayonnaise contain high-fructose corn syrup (HFCS). Fortunately, mayonnaise is quite easy to make at home, especially if you have a food processor. The trick lies in adding the oil very slowly. First, add a drop or two at a time, and then progress to a very thin stream while mixing the mayonnaise. If you don't have a food processor, you can whisk constantly instead, making sure you carefully pour the oil in a very thin stream. Use very fresh eggs or pasteurized eggs.

1 large egg yolk

1 tablespoon red wine vinegar

2 teaspoons freshly squeezed lemon juice

$\frac{1}{2}$ teaspoon sea salt

1 cup canola oil, light olive oil, or other neutral oil

1. In the bowl of a food processor, combine the egg yolk, vinegar, lemon juice, and sea salt. Turn on the food processor to combine.

2. With the food processor running, start adding the oil, one drop at a time, through the feed tube. After about 20 drops of oil, start adding the remaining oil in a very thin stream with the food processor still running.

3. Serve immediately, or store in a tightly sealed container in the refrigerator for up to 1 week.

Makes 1 cup / **Per Serving (2 tablespoons)**   Calories: 115   Protein: 0 grams
Sugar: 0 grams   Fat: 10 grams

INGREDIENT VARIATION

To make Garlic Mayonnaise, replace the canola oil with Garlic Oil (page 220).

Caesar Salad Dressing

NUT-FREE   VEGETARIAN   SOY-FREE

Prep time: 5 minutes   **Cook time:** None

Traditional Caesar salad dressing is not allowed on the FODMAP diet because it contains garlic. This recipe replaces chopped garlic with homemade garlic mayonnaise. Toss this dressing with shredded romaine lettuce and Parmesan cheese to make a delicious Caesar salad. Anchovy paste is optional, but it does add tremendous flavor to the dressing.

  2 tablespoons freshly squeezed lemon juice

  1 teaspoon Dijon mustard

  1 teaspoon Worcestershire sauce

  1 teaspoon anchovy paste (optional)

  1 cup Garlic Mayonnaise (page 224)

  1 ounce grated Parmesan cheese

  $\frac{1}{4}$ teaspoon sea salt

  $\frac{1}{4}$ teaspoon freshly ground black pepper

1. In a small bowl, whisk together the lemon juice, mustard, Worcestershire sauce, and anchovy paste (if using). Whisk in the mayonnaise until smooth. Stir in the Parmesan cheese, salt, and pepper.

2. Serve immediately, or store in a tightly sealed container in the refrigerator for up to 1 week.

Makes 1¼ cups / **Per Serving (2 tablespoons)**   Calories: 103   Protein: 1 gram
Sugar: 2 grams   Fat: 9 grams

Ranch Dressing

NUT-FREE   VEGETARIAN   SOY-FREE

Prep time: 10 minutes   **Cook time:** None

Ranch dressing is a classic American favorite, but sadly the buttermilk and garlic contain FODMAPs. This version uses homemade low-FODMAP versions of buttermilk and garlic mayonnaise and fresh herbs. If you're out of fresh herbs, replace 1 teaspoon of each fresh herb with $\frac{1}{2}$ teaspoon dried herbs. Let the ranch dressing sit in the refrigerator for a day to allow the flavors to mellow before using.

$\frac{3}{4}$ cups lactose-free whole milk

$\frac{3}{4}$ tablespoons freshly squeezed lemon juice

$\frac{1}{4}$ cup Garlic Mayonnaise (page 224)

1 teaspoon finely chopped fresh chives

1 teaspoon finely chopped fresh dill

1 teaspoon finely chopped fresh tarragon

$\frac{1}{2}$ teaspoon Dijon mustard

Dash cayenne pepper

1. In a small bowl, combine the milk and lemon juice. Allow the mixture to stand for 5 minutes, until it appears curdled.

2. Place the milk mixture, mayonnaise, herbs, mustard, and cayenne in the bowl of a food processor or blender. Blend until well combined.

3. Serve immediately, or store in a tightly sealed container in the refrigerator for up to 1 week.

Makes 1 cup / **Per Serving (2 tablespoons)**   Calories: 41   Protein: 1 gram
Sugar: 1 gram   Fat: 3 grams

Low-FODMAP Ketchup

Prep time: 5 minutes   **Cook time:** 5 minutes

Store-bought ketchup is high in FODMAPs because it contains onions, high-fructose corn syrup (HFCS), and garlic. This ketchup is moderate in FODMAPs, so it is essential that you limit your intake to no more than 1 tablespoon per day.

$1/2$ cup tomato paste

2 tablespoons Garlic Oil (page 220)

$1/4$ cup water

$1/4$ cup red wine vinegar

2 tablespoons dark brown sugar

$1/4$ teaspoon sea salt

$1/4$ teaspoon ground allspice

$1/4$ teaspoon ground cinnamon

Dash cayenne pepper

1. In a small saucepan over medium-high heat, combine the tomato paste, garlic oil, water, vinegar, dark brown sugar, salt, allspice, cinnamon, and cayenne and bring the mixture to a simmer.

2. Simmer, stirring constantly, until the sugar is completely dissolved, about 4 minutes. Serve immediately, or store in a tightly sealed container in the refrigerator for up to 2 weeks.

Makes 1¼ cups / **Per Serving (1 tablespoon)**   Calories: 21   Protein: 0 grams
Sugar: 2 grams   Fat: 1. 4 grams

Low-FODMAP Barbecue Sauce

NUT-FREE   VEGETARIAN   VEGAN   DAIRY-FREE   SOY-FREE

Prep time: 10 minutes   **Cook time:** 10 minutes

This low-FODMAP barbecue sauce is perfect for the pulled pork on page 189. You can also brush it on burgers or chicken while grilling them. It is tangy and sweet with just a hint of smoke.

$1/2$ cup tomato sauce

1 cup red wine vinegar

3 tablespoons brown sugar

1 tablespoon Dijon mustard

1 tablespoon Worcestershire sauce

$1/4$ teaspoon liquid smoke

1 tablespoon smoked paprika

1 teaspoon sea salt

1 teaspoon freshly ground black pepper

$1/4$ teaspoon cayenne pepper

2 tablespoons cornstarch

$1/4$ cup water

1. In a medium-sized saucepan, heat the tomato sauce, red wine vinegar, brown sugar, Dijon mustard, Worcestershire sauce, liquid smoke, smoked paprika, salt, pepper, and cayenne over medium-high until the mixture begins to simmer. Simmer, stirring frequently, for 5 minutes.

2. In a small bowl, whisk together the cornstarch and water.

3. Whisk the cornstarch slurry into the barbecue sauce. Return it to a simmer and cook until the sauce thickens, 2 to 3 minutes. Serve immediately, or store in a tightly sealed container in the refrigerator for up to 2 weeks.

Makes 2 cups / **Per Serving (2 tablespoons)**   Calories: 17   Protein: 0 grams
Sugar: 2 grams   Fat: 0 grams

Béchamel Sauce

Prep time: 5 minutes   **Cook time:** 20 minutes

Béchamel is one of the essential French "mother sauces." It is a white sauce that serves as the base for other sauces such as Alfredo sauce and cheese sauce for macaroni. This low-FODMAP béchamel sauce recipe includes a few variations that can be tossed with gluten-free pasta.

5 tablespoons unsalted butter

4 tablespoons gluten-free all-purpose flour

4 cups lactose-free whole milk

2 teaspoons salt

$\frac{1}{4}$ teaspoon freshly grated nutmeg

1. In a medium-sized saucepan, heat the butter over medium heat until it melts. Whisk in the flour, stirring frequently, until the mixture is light gold in color, about 7 minutes.

2. While the roux cooks, heat the milk in another medium-sized saucepan over medium heat until it simmers.

3. Whisking constantly, add the hot milk to the roux until it thickens and becomes smooth. Continue cooking, stirring constantly, for 8 minutes. ➤

Béchamel Sauce continued

4. Remove the sauce from the heat and stir in the salt and nutmeg. Serve.

....

Makes 4 cups / **Per Serving (½ cup)**   Calories: 141. 5   Protein: 4. 5 grams
Sugar: 6 grams   Fat: 10 grams

INGREDIENT VARIATIONS

To make Alfredo sauce, reduce the butter to 2 tablespoons and add 3 table-spoons Garlic Oil (page 220). Whisk in ½ cup grated Parmesan cheese at the end of cooking, just until the cheese melts and blends. Serve immediately.

To make cheese sauce for macaroni, whisk in ¼ cup grated sharp cheddar cheese and ¼ cup grated medium-sharp cheddar cheese at the end of cooking, just until the cheese melts and blends. Serve immediately.

Appendix A: 10 Tips for Eating Out

Dining out in restaurants can be stressful on a low-FODMAP eating plan. Fortunately, there's plenty you can do to ensure you don't irritate your IBS when you eat out.

1. **Plan ahead.** Most restaurants post their menus online. Many chain restaurants even list ingredients and nutritional information. You can also call the restaurant ahead of time to ask about their ingredients. Planning ahead can save you from feeling like the Spanish Inquisition when it's time to place your order.

2. **Tell the waiter your dietary restrictions.** Often, waitstaff (and even the chef) will be willing to work with you if you have food restrictions. Tell your server what your restrictions are and ask for recommendations.

3. **Ask questions about the menu.** Don't be afraid to ask questions about the menu. If the server doesn't know what's in a dish, he or she can ask the chef.

4. **Visit the restaurant away from peak hours.** Servers and chefs are typically much more willing and able to work with special dietary requests when they aren't slammed with other customers.

5. **Order simple menu items.** For example, you're less likely to encounter FODMAPs if you order a steak, steamed vegetables, and baked potatoes than you are if you order something that requires more work such as a soup, sauce, stew, or risotto.

6. **Don't assume a food is safe.** Even if you've ordered something simple such as a steak and baked potato, you need to make sure it hasn't been cooked with common ingredients like onions or garlic. Ask before ordering, and then ask again when it is delivered to the table.

7. **If your order is incorrect, don't be afraid to send it back.** Learn how to politely assert your dietary needs.

8. **If you order a salad, don't order it with dressing.** Instead, ask for oil and vinegar on the side and combine them yourself.

9. **Use a low-FODMAP smartphone app.** These apps can help you double-check ingredients you are unsure about.

10. **Order items à la carte.** If there are no composed dishes that will suit your diet, order a few sides, a salad, or appetizers that will. By ordering à la carte, you can create a balanced meal that meets your dietary needs.

Appendix B: Conversion Tables

Volume Equivalents (Liquid)

US STANDARD	US STANDARD (OUNCES)	METRIC (APPROXIMATE)
2 tablespoons	1 fl. oz.	30 mL
¼ cup	2 fl. oz.	60 mL
½ cup	4 fl. oz.	120 mL
1 cup	8 fl. oz.	240 mL
1½ cups	12 fl. oz.	355 mL
2 cups or 1 pint	16 fl. oz.	475 mL
4 cups or 1 quart	32 fl. oz.	1 L
1 gallon	128 fl. oz.	4 L

Oven Temperatures

FAHRENHEIT (F)	CELSIUS (C) (APPROXIMATE)
250	120
300	150
325	165
350	180
375	190
400	200
425	220
450	230

Volume Equivalents (Dry)

US STANDARD	METRIC (APPROXIMATE)
⅛ teaspoon	.5 mL
¼ teaspoon	1 mL
½ teaspoon	2 mL
¾ teaspoon	4 mL
1 teaspoon	5 mL
1 tablespoon	15 mL
¼ cup	59 mL
⅓ cup	79 mL
½ cup	118 mL
⅔ cup	156 mL
¾ cup	177 mL
1 cup	235 mL
2 cups or 1 pint	475 mL
3 cups	700 mL
4 cups or 1 quart	1 L
½ gallon	2 L
1 gallon	4 L

Weight Equivalents

US STANDARD	METRIC (APPROXIMATE)
½ ounce	15 g
1 ounce	30 g
2 ounces	60 g
4 ounces	115 g
8 ounces	225 g
12 ounces	340 g
16 ounces or 1 pound	455 g

Appendix C The Dirty Dozen and The Clean Fifteen

THE DIRTY DOZEN

Apples

Celery

Cherry
 tomatoes

Cucumbers

Grapes

Imported
 nectarines

Peaches

Potatoes

Imported snap
 peas

Spinach

Strawberries

Sweet bell
 peppers

plus

Hot peppers

Kale/collards

Each year, the Environmental Working Group, an environmental organization based in the United States, publishes a list they call "The Dirty Dozen." These are the fruits and vegetables that, when conventionally grown using chemical pesticides and fertilizers, carry the highest residues. If organically grown isn't an option for you, simply avoid these fruits and vegetables altogether. The list is updated each year, but here is the most recent list (2014).

Similarly, the Environmental Working Group publishes a list of "The Clean Fifteen," fruits and vegetables that, even when conventionally grown, contain very low levels of chemical pesticide or fertilizer residue. These items are acceptable to purchase conventionally grown.

You might want to snap a photo of these two lists and keep them on your phone to reference while shopping. Or you can download the Environmental Working Group's app to your phone or tablet.

THE CLEAN FIFTEEN

Asparagus

Avocados

Cabbage

Cantaloupe

Cauliflower

Eggplant

Grapefruit

Kiwis

Mangoes

Onions

Papayas

Pineapples

Sweet corn

Sweet peas
 (frozen)

Sweet potatoes

Resources

The following resources will help you stay abreast of the latest low-FODMAP research.

Books

Angelone, Anne. *The FODMAP-Free Paleo Breakthrough: 4 Weeks of Autoimmune Paleo Recipes without FODMAPs*. Seattle, WA: CreateSpace, 2013.

Catsos, Patsy. *Flavor without FODMAPs Cookbook: Love the Foods That Love You Back*. Portland, ME: Pond Cove Press, 2014.

Catsos, Patsy. *IBS-Free at Last! Change Your Carbs, Change Your Life with the FODMAP Elimination Diet*. Portland, ME: Pond Cove Press, 2012.

The FODMAP Solution: A Low-FODMAP Diet Plan and Cookbook to Manage IBS and Improve Digestion. Berkeley, CA: Shasta Press, 2014.

Nott, Natalie, and Geoff Nott. *The Low-FODMAP Cookbook*. Mitcham, Australia: Natalie Nott, 2012.

Perazzini, Suzanne. *Low-FODMAP Menus for Irritable Bowl Syndrome: Menus for Those on a Low-FODMAP Diet*. Seattle, WA: CreateSpace, 2014.

Scarlata, Kate. *The Complete Idiot's Guide to Eating Well with IBS*. New York, NY: Alpha Books, 2010.

Shepherd, Sue. *The Low-FODMAP Diet Cookbook: 150 Simple, Flavorful, Gut-Friendly Recipes to Ease the Symptoms of IBS*. New York, NY: The Experiment, 2014.

Shepherd, Sue, Peter Gibson, and William D. Chey. *The Complete Low-FODMAP Diet: A Revolutionary Plan for Managing IBS and Other Digestive Disorders*. New York, NY: The Experiment, 2013.

Websites

Monash University's *Low-FODMAP Diet for Irritable Bowel Syndrome*
http://www.med.monash.edu/cecs/gastro/fodmap

IBS Diets FODMAP Dieting Guide
www.ibsdiets.org/fodmap-diet/fodmap-food-list

IBS, FODMAP Diet, Celiac & Diabetes Counseling by Kate Scarlata, R.D.
http://www.katescarlata.com

Shepherd Works' *Low-FODMAP Diet* by Dr. Sue Shepherd
http://shepherdworks.com.au/disease-information/low-fodmap-diet

Stanford University's *Low-FODMAP Diet*
http://fodmapliving.com/the-science/stanford-university-low-fodmap-diet/

Tools and Apps

Monash University's *Low-FODMAP Diet App*
http://www.lowfodmap.com/monash-university-fodmap-diet-app

Low-FODMAP IBS Diet App
http://itunes.apple.com/us/app/low-fodmap-ibs-diet/id569607899?mt=8

References

De Roest, R. H., B. R. Dobbs, B. A. Chapman, B. Batman, L. A. O'Brien, J. A. Leeper, C. R. Hebblewaite, and R. B. Gearry. "The Low-FODMAP Diet Improves Gastrointestinal Symptoms in Patients with Irritable Bowel Syndrome: A Prospective Study." *The International Journal of Clinical Practice.* Volume 67, Issue 9 (May 2013): 895–903. doi:10.1111/ijcp.12128.

Environmental Working Group. "EWG's 2014 Shopper's Guide to Pesticides in Produce." Accessed May 14, 2014.http://www.ewg.org/release/ewgs-2014 -shoppers-guide-pesticides-produce.

Hyman, Mark. "Three Hidden Ways Wheat Makes You Fat." *Huffington Post.* Accessed May 6, 2014. http://www.huffingtonpost.com/dr-mark-hyman /wheat-gluten_b_1274872.html.

International Foundation for Functional and Gastrointestinal Disorders. "Facts about IBS." Accessed May 6, 2014. www.aboutibs.org/site/what-is-ibs/facts.

Li, James T. C. "Diseases and Conditions: Food Allergy: What's the Difference Between a Food Intolerance and a Food Allergy?" Mayo Clinic. Accessed May 6, 2014. http://www.mayoclinic.org/diseases-conditions/food-allergy/expert -answers/food-allergy/faq-20058538.

Mayo Clinic. "Diseases and Conditions: Inflammatory Bowel Disease." Accessed May 6, 2014. http://www.mayoclinic.org/diseases-conditions/inflammatory -bowel-disease/basics/definition/con-20034908.

National Foundation for Celiac Awareness. "Celiac Disease Facts and Figures." Accessed May 6, 2014. http://www.celiaccentral.org/celiac-disease/facts-and -figures.

Stanford Hospitals & Clinics. "The Low-FODMAP Diet." Accessed May 6, 2014. http://fodmapliving.com/wp-content/uploads/2013/02/Stanford -University-Low-FODMAP-Diet-Handout.pdf.

Sui, Yali, Gordana Djuras, and Gerhard M. Kostner. "Fructose Malabsorption
Influences Chronic and Recurrent Infectious Diseases, Dyspepsia, and
Heartburn." *The Open Gastroenterology Journal.* Volume 6 (2012): 1–7.
Accessed May 6, 2014. http://benthamscience.com/open/togasj/articles
/V006/1TOGASJ.pdf.

Thomas, J. Reggie, Rakesha Nanda, and Lin H. Shu, "A FODMAP Diet Update:
Craze or Credible?" Charlottesville, VA: University of Virginia School of
Medicine. Accessed May 6, 2014. http://www.medicine.virginia.edu/clinical
/departments/medicine/divisions/digestive-health/nutrition-support
-team/nutrition-articles/Parrish_Dec_12.pdf.

WebMD. "Irritable Bowel Syndrome (IBS) Health Center: Irritable Bowel
Syndrome (IBS) Triggers and Prevention." Accessed May 6, 2014.
http://www.webmd.com/ibs/guide/ibs-triggers-prevention-strategies.

Index

Photo credits:

Con Poulos/OffSet, p. ii; Keller & Keller Photography/Stockfood, p. 61; Izy Hossack/Stockfood, p.62; Leigh Beisch/Stockfood, p. 84; Olga Miltsova /Stockfood, p. 130; Teubner Foodfoto GmbH/Stockfood, p. 148; Christina Schmidhofer/Stockfood, p. 168; Elizabeth Watt/Stockfood, p. 194; Robert Morris/Stockfood, p. 219